THE 50 GREATEST
LOST TREASURES OF ALL TIME

❧ LOCHLAINN SEABROOK WRITES IN THE FOLLOWING GENRES ❧

Academic
Adventure
Alternate History
American Civil War
American History
American Politics
American South
American West
Anatomy and Physiology
Ancient History
Antiquities
Anthologies
Anthropology
Apocrypha
Aquariology
Archaeology
Art
Art History
Astronomy
Aviation
Aviation History
Behavioral Science
Biblical Exegesis
Biblical Hermeneutics
Bioarchaeology
Biography
Book History
Botany
Camping
Children's Books
Christian Mysticism
Clinical Studies
Coffee Table Books
Coloring Books
Comparative History
Comparative Mythology
Comparative Religion
Conservation
Constitutional Studies
Cooking
Cultural Anthropology
Cultural Geography
Cultural Heritage
Cultural Heritage Studies
Cultural History
Cultural Studies
Cultural Tourism
Cryptozoology
Deep Time Natural History
Destination Guides
Diet and Nutrition
Earth Sciences
Ecology
Ecotourism
Educational
Encyclopediography
Entertainment
Environmental History
Environmental Science
Environmental Studies
Environmental Tourism
Epistemology
Ethnobotany
Ethnology
Ethology
Ethnomusicology
Ethnic Studies
Etymology
European History
Evolutionary Anthropology
Evolutionary Biology
Evolutionary History
Evolutionary Psychology
Exploration
Exobiology

Exposés
Family Histories
Field Guides
Film
Folklore
Forestry
Genealogy
General Audience
Geography
Geology
Genetics
Ghost Stories
Gospels
Guidebooks
Handbooks
Health and Fitness
Heritage Conservation
Heritage Travel
Hiking
Historical Ecology
Historical Fiction
Historical Nonfiction
Historiography
History
History of Ideas
History of Medicine
History of Science
Hobbies and Crafts
Human Evolution
Humanities
Humor
Ichthyology
Illustrated Lost History
Illustrations
Inspirational
Illustrated Zoological Anthologies
Intellectual History
Interdisciplinary Lost Knowledge
Interviews
Journalism
Law of Attraction
Lexicography
Life After Death
Lifestyle
Literary History
Literature
Lost Intellectual Heritage
Lost Knowledge Studies
Lost Treasures
Marine Biology
Matriarchy
Medical History
Memoir
Men's Studies
Metahistory
Metaphysics
Military
Military History
Museum Studies
Mysteries and Enigmas
Mysticism
Mythology
National Parks
Natural Health
Natural History
Natural Philosophy
Natural Science
Nature
Nature Appreciation
Nature Art
Nonfiction
Oceanography
Onomastics
Outdoor Recreation
Paleoanthropology

Paleoecology
Paleography
Paleoichthyology
Paleontology
Paleozoology
Paranormal
Parapsychology
Parks & Campgrounds
Patriarchy
Patriotism
Performing Arts
Philosophy
Philosophy of Science
Photography
Physical Anthropology
Pictorial
Poetry
Politics
Prehistoric Art
Prehistoric Life
Prehistory
Preservation Studies
Presidential History
Primatology
Primary Documents
Prophecy
Psychology
Quiz
Quotations
Recollections
Reference
Religion
Revolutionary Period
Science
Scripture
Self-help
Social Sciences
Sociology
Southern Culture
Southern Heritage
Southern Narratives
Southern Studies
Southern Traditions
Speeches
Spirituality
Spiritualism
Sport Science
Symbolism
Technology
Thanatology
Thealogy
Theology
Theosophy
Tourism
Travel
UFOlogy
United States
Vanished Works Studies
Vexillology
Victorian Era Studies
Victorian Medicine
Visual Arts
Visual Cultural Memory Studies
Visual Encyclopediography
Visual Natural History
War
Western Civilization
Wildlife
Wildlife Biology
Wildlife Photography
Women's Studies
World History
Writing
Young Adult
Zoology

Mr. Seabrook does not author books for fame and glory, but for the love of writing and sharing his knowledge.

Be curious, not judgmental.

The 50 Greatest
LOST TREASURES
Of All Time

A Visual Guide to Humanity's Most Important Vanished Artifacts

LOCHLAINN SEABROOK
Bestselling Author, Award-winning Historian, Acclaimed Artist

Diligently Researched and Generously Illustrated by the Author for the Elucidation of the Reader

2025

Sea Raven Press, Park County, Wyoming USA

Published by
Sea Raven Press, LLC, founded 1995
Park County, Wyoming, USA
SeaRavenPress.com

All text, artwork, and illustrations copyright © Lochlainn Seabrook 2025
in accordance with U.S. and international copyright laws and regulations, as stated and protected under the Berne Union for the Protection of Literary and Artistic Property (Berne Convention), and the Universal Copyright Convention (the UCC). All rights reserved under the Pan-American and International Copyright Conventions.

PRINTING HISTORY
1st SRP paperback edition, 1st printing, December 2025 • ISBN: 978-1-955351-78-2
1st SRP hardcover edition, 1st printing, December 2025 • ISBN: 978-1-955351-79-9

ISBN: 978-1-955351-78-2 (paperback)
Library of Congress Control Number: 2026932432

This work is the copyrighted intellectual property of Lochlainn Seabrook and has been registered with the Copyright Office at the Library of Congress in Washington, D.C., USA. No part of this work (including text, covers, drawings, photos, illustrations, maps, images, diagrams, etc.), in whole or in part, may be used, reproduced, stored in a retrieval system, or transmitted, in any form or by any means now known or hereafter invented, without written permission from the publisher. The sale, duplication, hire, lending, copying, digitalization, or reproduction of this material, in any manner or form whatsoever, is also prohibited, and is a violation of federal, civil, and digital copyright law, which provides severe civil and criminal penalties for any violations.

The 50 Greatest Lost Treasures of All Time: A Visual Guide to Humanity's Most Important Vanished Artifacts, by Lochlainn Seabrook. Includes an introduction, notes to the reader, illustrations, and a bibliography.

ARTWORK
Front and back cover design and art, book design, layout, font selection, and interior art by Lochlainn Seabrook;
All images, pictures, photos, illustrations, image captions, graphic design, and graphic art copyright © Lochlainn Seabrook;
All images created and/or selected, placed, manipulated, cleaned, colored, and tinted by Lochlainn Seabrook;
Cover image: "The Lost Treasure of Caledonia," copyright © Lochlainn Seabrook;
All rights reserved.

All persons who approve of the authority and principles of Colonel Lochlainn Seabrook's literary work, and realize its benefits as a means of reeducating the world about facts left out of mainstream books, are hereby requested to avidly recommend his titles to others and to vigorously cooperate in extending their reach, scope, and influence around the globe.

The views documented in this book concerning some of the world's most spectacular lost treasures are those of the publisher.

PROUDLY WRITTEN, DESIGNED, AND PUBLISHED IN THE UNITED STATES OF AMERICA.

DEDICATION

To the guardians of forgotten knowledge–past, present, and yet to come.

Illustration copyright © Lochlainn Seabrook.

EPIGRAPH

"Antiquities are history defaced, or some remnants of history which have casually escaped the shipwreck of time."

Francis Bacon, 1625

Illustration copyright © Lochlainn Seabrook.

CONTENTS

Notes to the Reader ઺ page 11
Why the World's Lost Treasures Matter, by Lochlainn Seabrook ઺ page 12
Introduction, by Lochlainn Seabrook ઺ page 13

1. Amber Room ઺ page 16
2. Ark of the Covenant ઺ page 18
3. Arthur Conan Doyle Portrait ઺ page 20
4. Book of Kells Treasure Binding ઺ page 22
5. Book of Thoth ઺ page 24
6. Buddhist Sanskrit Sutras of Nalanda ઺ page 26
7. Celtic Gold of the Boudica Rebellion ઺ page 28
8. Charter of Atlantis ઺ page 30
9. Colossus of Rhodes ઺ page 32
10. Components of the Antikythera Mechanism ઺ page 34
11. Confederate Treasure ઺ page 36
12. Cook Expedition Journals ઺ page 38
13. Crown of the Welsh Princes ઺ page 40
14. Dead Sea Scrolls ઺ page 42
15. Denisovan Burial Treasure ઺ page 44
16. Dutchman's Gold Mine ઺ page 46
17. Emerald Tablet of Hermes Trismegistus ઺ page 48
18. Etruscan Gold Books ઺ page 50
19. Gnostic Gospels ઺ page 52
20. Gospel of the Hebrews ઺ page 54
21. Gospel of the Nazarenes ઺ page 56
22. Holy Grail ઺ page 58
23. Honjō Masamune ઺ page 60
24. Inca Gold of Atahualpa ઺ page 62
25. Knights Templar Treasure ઺ page 64
26. Leaves of the Beowulf Manuscript ઺ page 66
27. Library of Alexandria ઺ page 68
28. Maya Codices ઺ page 70
29. Menorah of the Second Temple ઺ page 72
30. Montezuma's Treasure ઺ page 74
31. Nazi Gold Hoard ઺ page 76
32. Nibelungen Hoard ઺ page 78
33. Norse Greenland Monastic Library ઺ page 80

34. Norse Sagas ❧ page 82
35. Original New Testament ❧ page 84
36. Palladium of Troy ❧ page 86
37. Plays of Shakespeare ❧ page 88
38. Poems of Sappho ❧ page 90
39. Polynesian Navigational Tablets ❧ page 92
40. Regalia of Charlemagne ❧ page 94
41. Roman Legion IX Scrolls ❧ page 96
42. Romanov Crown Jewels ❧ page 98
43. Scroll of Pytheas of Massalia ❧ page 100
44. Secret Gospel of Mark ❧ page 102
45. Sibylline Books ❧ page 104
46. Sumerian King Lists ❧ page 106
47. Templar Fleet ❧ page 108
48. Tomb of Cleopatra VII and Mark Antony ❧ page 110
49. Tomb of Genghis Khan ❧ page 112
50. Treasure of Lima ❧ page 114

Bibliography ❧ page 116
Meet the Author-Historian-Artist ❧ page 133
Praise for the Author-Historian-Artist ❧ page 135
Learn More ❧ page 139

Illustration copyright © Lochlainn Seabrook.

Notes to the Reader

MY SOURCES
☛ This book, like all of my historical works, is grounded in primary documents, respected scholarly studies, archaeological records, and the earliest available accounts. The intention throughout is accuracy, balance, and objectivity. Speculative claims, legends, and later embellishments are included only when historically relevant and are clearly framed as such.

SCHOLARLY CONSENSUS
☛ The world of lost treasures is defined by missing evidence, disputed narratives, and partial or damaged records. Because the surviving material is often fragmentary or contradictory, historians rarely agree on every detail. Differences in measurements, locations, chronologies, and descriptions among reputable sources are to be expected. Where uncertainty persists, I have drawn on the strongest and most credible data, noting when an estimate or interpretive judgment is required. Accordingly, most of my illustrations in this volume are necessarily dramatized, symbolic, idealized, or atmospheric, due to the absence of definitive visual documentation.

ON LEGENDS & LATER TRADITIONS
☛ Many lost treasures carry centuries of folklore, conjecture, and mythic retellings. These traditions are included only when they help illuminate a treasure's historical influence, cultural significance, or interpretive legacy. They are not presented as established fact unless supported by reliable evidence.

DISCLAIMER
☛ The images of human figures in this work are fictional representations created solely for artistic purposes. Any resemblance to actual individuals is unintentional.

WHY THE WORLD'S LOST TREASURES MATTER

The study of the world's lost treasures is far more than a search for missing objects. It is an exploration of humanity's collective memory. Each vanished artifact—whether a room of carved amber, a scroll consumed by fire, or a relic spirited away by war—carries with it a portion of our cultural identity. When we investigate these absences, we are actually studying the forces that shaped civilizations: ambition, belief, conflict, curiosity, and the inherently fragile nature of recorded history.

Lost treasures illuminate the limits of human knowledge. They remind us that even the greatest achievements can be erased by time, disaster, or deliberate destruction. By understanding how and why these items disappeared, we gain insight into the vulnerabilities of our own era. This perspective encourages a deeper appreciation of the texts, artworks, and artifacts that have survived against all odds, emphasizing the responsibility we carry to preserve the world's remaining heritage.

The search for lost treasures also strengthens interdisciplinary thinking. Historians, archaeologists, linguists, theologians, scientists, artists, and explorers all bring different tools to the same mystery. Their combined work forms a richer, more complete view of the past. In a world where knowledge is often compartmentalized, lost treasures provide a rare arena where multiple fields intersect naturally, each revealing a new dimension of the story.

Most importantly, these mysteries inspire. They invite us to imagine what still lies hidden—beneath ruins, behind sealed archives, under coral reefs, or in the unexamined corners of ancient history. They remind us that the past is not fully written, that there are chapters still waiting to be uncovered. For readers, researchers, and seekers of truth, lost treasures ignite the essential human drive to know more, to look deeper, and to broaden our sense of what might yet be found.

In this way, studying the world's lost treasures becomes a journey of both recovery and discovery: a way to understand what humanity once valued, what it failed to protect, and what it still hopes to reclaim. L.S.

INTRODUCTION

Throughout my life as an author, historian, artist, and explorer, I have naturally been drawn to the world's great lost treasures—the masterpieces, archives, inventions, and cultural riches that once existed, but which have since vanished into oblivion. These losses are far more than mere historical curiosities. They are markers of our shared human story, reminders that knowledge and beauty are fragile, and proof that even the greatest achievements can disappear in a moment through war, disaster, neglect, or the simple passage of time.

My book, *The 50 Greatest Lost Treasures of All Time*, gathers many of the most compelling missing valuables ever recorded, chosen for their historical weight, cultural influence, and the lasting impact of their disappearance. Some were central to entire civilizations; others shaped religion, literature, statecraft, and scientific progress. A few survive only through fragments, descriptions, or scattered eyewitness accounts. Yet even those traces reveal the depth of what has been lost.

My goal here is simple: to present these treasures with clarity, accuracy, and respect. Each entry distills what the item was, why it mattered, the circumstances of its loss, and what modern research suggests about its fate. When evidence is disputed, I outline the major positions without embellishment. When details are uncertain, I say so plainly. This approach reflects my lifelong dedication to truthful, careful scholarship across all my work—whether writing, filming, illustrating, or documenting the natural and historical world.

Lost treasures captivate us because they represent unfinished chapters. What wisdom burned with the Library of Alexandria? What brilliance was contained in the Book of Thoth? Where are the Honjō Masamune, Boudica's Celtic gold hoard, the missing Maya codices, and the lost journals of Cook's expedition? These mysteries endure not just because they are romantic, but because they remind us that our history is incomplete—and always will be.

By exploring what is gone, we gain a clearer understanding of humanity's creative reach and the responsibility we share to preserve what remains. It is my hope that this book deepens that sense of connection, curiosity, and stewardship as we revisit some of the greatest treasures the world has lost.

Lochlainn Seabrook
Park County, Wyoming, USA
December 2025

"Books invite all; they constrain none."
Hartley Burr Alexander (1873-1939)

The Greatest
LOST TREASURES
of All Time

AMBER ROOM

TYPE: Baroque decorative chamber composed of carved amber panels, gold leaf, mirrors, and gilded ornamentation created for a Prussian royal interior.
ORIGIN: Designed by German and Danish craftsmen for the Berlin City Palace and later transferred to Russia for installation in the Catherine Palace at Tsarskoye Selo.
DATE / PERIOD: Constructed between circa 1701 and 1710 and expanded in the mid-18th Century.
DESCRIPTION: A luminous amber-paneled room covering roughly 180 square feet of wall surface, featuring intarsia, relief work, mirrors, and gilded architectural elements. Its panels incorporated thousands of individually cut amber pieces set over wooden substrates.
SIGNIFICANCE: Recognized as one of the greatest achievements of European decorative art and a symbol of Prussian–Russian diplomatic ties.
WHAT HAPPENED: German forces dismantled and removed the room in 1941, installed it in Königsberg Castle, and crated it during late 1944 as Allied bombing approached. The panels vanished during the collapse of East Prussia.
PRIMARY SOURCES: Prussian and Russian court inventories, construction records, Königsberg exhibition documentation, and wartime transport lists.
POSSIBLE SURVIVING FRAGMENTS: Small decorative amber pieces, gilded mounts, and period photographs preserved in Russian and European archives.
LOCATION LAST KNOWN: Stored within Königsberg Castle in East Prussia in late 1944.
STATUS: Completely lost since World War II, with no authenticated fragments confirmed.
REDISCOVERY EFFORTS: Archival research, site excavations, and searches of bunkers and wartime repositories have been conducted since the late 1940s.
NOTABLE QUOTATIONS ABOUT IT: Described in early modern and modern accounts as an unparalleled achievement of amber artistry.
LEGACY: Remains a prominent example of wartime cultural loss and inspired the full-scale reconstruction completed at Tsarskoye Selo in 2003. A lost treasure that highlights the vulnerability of large-scale decorative works during conflict. Its reconstruction sustains scholarly interest in early modern amber craftsmanship; an outstanding example of the fragility of cultural heritage.

Eighteenth-Century court visitor standing within the famed but now lost amber-laden chamber at Tsarskoye Selo circa 1760, illustrating its role as a ceremonial showpiece of imperial craftsmanship. Illustration copyright © Lochlainn Seabrook.

ARK OF THE COVENANT

TYPE: A sacred Israelite cult object described as a gold-covered acacia chest containing covenantal tablets. Its construction, transport, and ritual role are preserved in ancient Hebrew texts.

ORIGIN: Formed within the early religious structure of ancient Israel and attributed to Bezalel under priestly instruction. Its design reflects a developed priestly tradition with defined ritual guidelines and a centralized cultic system.

DATE / PERIOD: Placed by most scholarship in the late 2nd Millennium BC during the formative Israelite period.

DESCRIPTION: A wood chest overlaid with gold, fitted with poles, and topped by a gold lid called the kapporet. Two golden cherubim framed a symbolic throne space associated with divine presence. Its proportions and ornamentation are known solely through preserved textual specifications that detail one of antiquity's most distinctive ritual objects.

SIGNIFICANCE: Served as ancient Israel's central sacred object and represented the covenantal bond with its deity. Functioned as a ritual, symbolic, and political focus shaping worship, legal identity, and communal cohesion across successive generations.

WHAT HAPPENED: Its ultimate fate is unrecorded. It is last firmly situated in First Temple accounts before the Babylonian conquest in the early 6th Century BC, after which no authoritative source confirms its survival or relocation.

PRIMARY SOURCES: Hebrew Bible passages in Exodus, Numbers, Deuteronomy, Joshua, Samuel, Kings, and Chronicles. Josephus comments on its absence in the Second Temple era and preserves earlier tradition.

POSSIBLE SURVIVING FRAGMENTS: None are known. No claims of extant components have been authenticated through primary documentation or archaeological study.

LOCATION LAST KNOWN: The First Temple in Jerusalem shortly before its destruction, circa 588–587 BC.

STATUS: Lost since antiquity with no verified recoveries.

REDISCOVERY EFFORTS: Archaeologists and textual scholars have examined First Temple strata, exilic sources, and regional traditions, but all investigations remain inconclusive.

NOTABLE QUOTATIONS ABOUT IT: Hebrew texts emphasize its centrality to covenantal worship. Josephus noted its absence in later ritual and its historical significance.

LEGACY: The Ark endures as a defining symbol of ancient Israelite faith and continues to influence religious thought, historical study, artistic representation, and cultural memory across millennia.

Temple attendant in the First Temple precinct circa 7th Century BCE, underscoring the ritual centrality of the Ark in Israel's early religious life. Illustration copyright © Lochlainn Seabrook.

ARTHUR CONAN DOYLE PORTRAIT

TYPE: A missing late 19th Century painted portrait of Sir Arthur Conan Doyle created by an unidentified British artist.
ORIGIN: Produced in Britain during Doyle's early literary prominence when commissioned portraiture was standard for both private display and public documentation.
DATE / PERIOD: Circa 1890–1900 during the rapid international ascent of Doyle's Sherlock Holmes stories.
DESCRIPTION: A traditional studio oil portrait depicting Doyle in formal Victorian attire with the composed professional bearing associated with influential authors of the era. The pose likely reflected contemporary portrait conventions emphasizing restraint and intellectual character.
SIGNIFICANCE: The work offered an early visual record of a literary figure whose detective fiction shaped global narrative technique and helped formalize deductive logic in popular culture. Its loss removes a primary artifact connecting Doyle's personal identity with one of the most important bodies of fiction in Western literature.
WHAT HAPPENED: The portrait disappeared after mid 20th Century changes in family holdings, inheritance transitions, and private relocations. Subsequent decades produced no trace of the painting in institutional records, published catalogues, or auction documentation.
PRIMARY SOURCES: Doyle family correspondence, early biographical references, and period notices confirm the portrait's existence and provide general descriptions of its character.
POSSIBLE SURVIVING FRAGMENTS: No authenticated fragments or photographs are known. A few unverified reproduction prints circulate privately minus verifiable provenance.
LOCATION LAST KNOWN: A private residence in southern England before vanishing from documented view.
STATUS: Lost, with no confirmed appearances in modern archival, academic, or market sources.
REDISCOVERY EFFORTS: Inquiries by collectors, Doyle scholars, and Holmesian societies have surfaced intermittently but have produced no substantiated lead.
NOTABLE QUOTATIONS ABOUT IT: No direct artistic commentary survives, though early writers noted the portrait as part of Doyle's formal public presentation.
LEGACY: Its disappearance limits visual scholarship on one of literature's most influential authors, leaving modern researchers with an incomplete record of his historical image.

A mysterious and unnamed Victorian artist touches up his painting of the widely celebrated writer Arthur Conan Doyle in a portrait now lost to time, circa 1895. Illustration copyright © Lochlainn Seabrook.

BOOK OF KELLS TREASURE BINDING

TYPE: Illuminated Gospel manuscript created in the Insular Celtic tradition.
ORIGIN: Produced by Irish monks of the Columban network, likely at Iona before relocation to Kells.
DATE / PERIOD: Circa late 8th to early 9th Century.
DESCRIPTION: A richly ornamented Latin Gospel Book containing the Four Gospels, prefatory material, carpet pages, incipit pages, and full-page Evangelist portraits. Its pigments, geometric precision, and minute interlace showcase an extraordinary level of artistic control that typifies the peak of Insular illumination.
SIGNIFICANCE: The manuscript reflects Ireland's Golden Age of Christian culture and demonstrates the synthesis of Celtic, Hiberno-Saxon, and Mediterranean influences. It remains one of the most important testimonies to early medieval monastic scholarship and artistic innovation. Its scale and complexity have made it a primary object of study in manuscript arts.
WHAT HAPPENED: In the year 1007 the manuscript was stolen from the Abbey of Kells during a period of regional turbulence. Medieval annals report that its ornate jeweled treasure binding was stripped off and never recovered. The manuscript itself was later found, but the vanished cover became one of Ireland's most enduring lost artifacts.
PRIMARY SOURCES: Annals of Ulster; Annals of Tigernach; Annals of the Four Masters; Columban monastic references.
POSSIBLE SURVIVING FRAGMENTS: No authenticated elements of the original treasure binding are known.
LOCATION LAST KNOWN: In or near Kells, County Meath, Ireland, at the time of the 1007 theft.
STATUS: Binding lost and unverified by mainstream scholarship, though its disappearance is firmly recorded.
REDISCOVERY EFFORTS: Antiquarians, archaeologists, and manuscript specialists have reviewed Viking hoards, ecclesiastical inventories, and regional discoveries, yet no fragment consistent with the binding has emerged.
NOTABLE QUOTATIONS ABOUT IT: The Annals of Ulster call it "the great Gospel of Colum Cille," highlighting its sanctity and exceptional workmanship.
LEGACY: The Book of Kells remains a global emblem of Insular art. Its missing treasure binding is considered one of Ireland's greatest cultural losses, a legendary masterpiece whose disappearance continues to inspire scholarly debate.

Early medieval artisanship associated with the vanished Book of Kells treasure binding, circa 800 A.D. Illustration copyright © Lochlainn Seabrook.

BOOK OF THOTH

TYPE: A legendary Egyptian sacred text attributed to the god Thoth and said to contain divine knowledge of ritual, creation, medicine, and cosmic order. It functioned in antiquity as the archetype of priestly wisdom literature.

ORIGIN: Rooted in Pharaonic temple culture, especially centers linked to Thoth such as Hermopolis, where scribes, astronomers, and ritualists preserved esoteric knowledge.

DATE / PERIOD: Traditionally placed between the late Old Kingdom and the New Kingdom, with the mythic form fixed by the 1st Millennium BC and referenced into the Ptolemaic era.

DESCRIPTION: Described as a multi-section compendium granting mastery of divine speech, ritual formulas, healing knowledge, and celestial laws. Ancient sources mention hymns, magical texts, astronomical tables, and instructions governing temple rites and sacred communication.

SIGNIFICANCE: It represented the pinnacle of Egyptian sacerdotal learning, uniting theology, magic, and cosmology, and its loss removed a key witness to the intellectual canon that later shaped the ancient spiritual-philosophical system Hermetism.

WHAT HAPPENED: Greco-Roman accounts report that priests hid or destroyed copies due to the text's dangerous power. Later upheavals, temple closures, and library losses likely eliminated surviving exemplars.

PRIMARY SOURCES: Referenced in Demotic tales, Ptolemaic ritual literature, the Greek Hermetica, and classical authors including Plutarch and Clement of Alexandria.

POSSIBLE SURVIVING FRAGMENTS: Certain Demotic ritual papyri and early Hermetic dialogues preserve thematic parallels but cannot be authenticated as parts of the original work.

LOCATION LAST KNOWN: Said to have been kept in a sealed container within a restricted temple chamber under priestly protection.

STATUS: Lost. No confirmed manuscript has ever been identified.

REDISCOVERY EFFORTS: Egyptologists and historians of Hermetism compare extant ritual papyri and cosmological texts for structural links, but none match the ancient descriptions.

NOTABLE QUOTATIONS ABOUT IT: Classical writers described it as a book containing the speech by which the gods created all things.

LEGACY: The Book of Thoth influenced Hermetism, Western esotericism, and scholarly models of Egyptian intellectual life, remaining an emblem of vanished sacred knowledge.

Priestly scholar consulting a revered temple manuscript linked to Thoth's forbidden and now lost teachings, circa 1200 BCE. Illustration copyright © Lochlainn Seabrook.

BUDDHIST SANSKRIT SUTRAS OF NALANDA

TYPE: Religious texts, manuscript corpus, monastic university library holdings.
ORIGIN: Nalanda Mahavihara in the Magadha region of northeastern India, produced and copied by scholar-monks of major Mahayana and Vajrayana traditions.
DATE / PERIOD: Mainly 5th–12th Centuries, with antecedent material grounded in earlier Buddhist literature.
DESCRIPTION: These manuscripts were preserved within Nalanda Mahavihara, a monastic university complex with scriptoria and multi-story libraries; its palm-leaf Sanskrit sutras, commentaries, ritual texts, and scholastic treatises formed the core of its curriculum.
SIGNIFICANCE: Nalanda's sutra collection shaped Buddhist philosophy across Asia and preserved intellectual lineages central to Mahayana and Vajrayana thought.
WHAT HAPPENED: Nalanda was destroyed during late 12th-Century invasions, culminating in the 1193 attack under Bakhtiyar Khalji, when fires consumed monastic buildings and extensive manuscript repositories.
PRIMARY SOURCES: Xuanzang and Yijing documented the scale of Nalanda's scriptural holdings, while Tibetan historians such as Taranatha preserved references to numerous lost works.
POSSIBLE SURVIVING FRAGMENTS: Scattered Sanskrit folios in Nepal and Central Asia may relate to Nalanda's corpus, with several works preserved only through Tibetan or Chinese translations.
LOCATION LAST KNOWN: Nalanda Mahavihara, present-day Bihar, India.
STATUS: Lost, with no complete Sanskrit manuscripts from the original collection surviving.
REDISCOVERY EFFORTS: Scholars compare surviving fragments with Asian translations to recover elements of vanished texts, an ongoing process that continues to refine our understanding.
NOTABLE QUOTATIONS ABOUT IT: Xuanzang and Yijing described Nalanda's libraries as vast and unmatched.
LEGACY: The sutras influenced Buddhist doctrine and intellectual history; their destruction remains a major loss to India's scholarly heritage. Their disappearance also marks a critical break in the preservation of India's classical Buddhist manuscript culture and continues to shape modern interpretations of India's Buddhist past.

Buddhist monk examining palm-leaf sutras associated with the later-destroyed Nalanda Mahavihara manuscripts in a scriptoria chamber in Bihar, AD 5th–12th Century. Illustration copyright © Lochlainn Seabrook.

CELTIC GOLD OF THE BOUDICA REBELLION

TYPE: A concentrated body of Iceni gold ornaments, torcs, votive fittings, and coinage associated with the Boudican uprising against Rome.

ORIGIN: Created by Celtic craftsmen in eastern Britain within the Iceni cultural tradition, noted for refined metalworking and symbolic elite regalia.

DATE / PERIOD: Early to mid-1st Century AD during the final years of autonomous Iceni authority and the Roman suppression of the revolt.

DESCRIPTION: The treasure included elite torcs, armlets, disc ornaments, and gold coins shaped with twisted rods and repoussé imagery used to denote lineage and ceremonial rank.

SIGNIFICANCE: These items embodied Iceni wealth and political legitimacy and aided understanding of high-status metallurgy in Iron Age Britain.

WHAT HAPPENED: The gold vanished during Roman reprisals when confiscation, looting, emergency concealment, and the destruction of tribal strongholds dispersed or eliminated identifiable caches.

PRIMARY SOURCES: Tacitus and Cassius Dio record the seizure of Iceni wealth and punitive measures enacted during and after the revolt.

POSSIBLE SURVIVING FRAGMENTS: A few Iceni gold items in British collections share stylistic traits with elite regalia, but cannot be securely connected to rebellion-era deposits.

LOCATION LAST KNOWN: Iceni territory in present-day Norfolk and Suffolk near major tribal centers around Venta Icenorum.

STATUS: Unverified by mainstream scholarship but referenced in Roman accounts documenting confiscated or concealed Iceni valuables tied to the uprising.

REDISCOVERY EFFORTS: Regional excavations and metal-detecting across East Anglia have produced isolated gold pieces but no confirmed rebellion-linked hoard.

NOTABLE QUOTATIONS ABOUT IT: Tacitus cites Roman expropriation as prompting "just causes of war," while Cassius Dio describes widespread plunder as the province was subdued.

LEGACY: The lost gold represents the extinguished autonomy of the Iceni, one of a number of cultural traditions erased from Celtic-Brittonic history under Roman consolidation.

Iceni Queen Boudica and her two daughters during the tense prelude to the revolt of A.D. 60–61. The modern search continues for the tribe's lost priceless gold hoard. Illustration copyright © Lochlainn Seabrook.

CHARTER OF ATLANTIS

TYPE: An ancient geopolitical record describing the laws, administrative structure, and territorial organization of Atlantis.

ORIGIN: Said to have been stored in the Temple of Neith at Saïs, where Egyptian priests preserved long historical registers.

DATE / PERIOD: Attributed to a remote era predating Classical Greece by many millennia, later summarized for Solon in the 6th Century BC and conveyed to Plato in the 4th Century BC.

DESCRIPTION: The Lost Charter of Atlantis outlined the island's confederated government, its division among ten royal houses, and the obligations of each ruler under a central authority. It described the capital's circular harbors, agricultural systems, military resources, and relations with neighboring regions. It also recounted Atlantean expansion into parts of Europe and North Africa.

SIGNIFICANCE: The charter formed the Egyptian basis of Plato's account and became one of antiquity's most influential missing documents. It preserved a rare transmission of deep-time history and shaped later discussions of governance, imperial overreach, and environmental decline.

WHAT HAPPENED: The record was likely lost during the decline of regional priesthoods, the destruction of temple libraries under later foreign rule, and the collapse of Late Period archival systems. No manuscript is known to have survived transitional administrative eras.

PRIMARY SOURCES: Plato's *Timaeus* and *Critias*, preserving Solon's summary of the Saïs narrative.

POSSIBLE SURVIVING FRAGMENTS: Only the excerpts embedded in Plato's dialogues, representing a secondary witness, not the primary document.

LOCATION LAST KNOWN: Temple of Neith, Saïs, western Nile Delta, Egypt.

STATUS: Lost, with no confirmed fragment in Egyptian, Greek, or later archaeological collections.

REDISCOVERY EFFORTS: Scholars have examined king lists, Late Period inscriptions, and Classical testimonies, but none align with the detailed account attributed to the Saïs archive.

NOTABLE QUOTATIONS ABOUT IT: A Saïs priest told Solon that Egyptian archives preserved written accounts of ancient nations and earlier catastrophes "kept in our temples and preserved for ages."

LEGACY: The charter remains central to the Atlantis tradition and continues to influence studies of early statecraft, cultural transmission, and the preservation of remote historical memory.

Egyptian scribe reviewing a hieratic record linked to the now-lost Temple Library of Neith in Saïs, Late Period Egypt (664–332 BC). Illustration copyright © Lochlainn Seabrook.

COLOSSUS OF RHODES

TYPE: A lost monumental bronze sculpture revered in antiquity as a triumph of Hellenistic engineering and artistic mastery.
ORIGIN: Created on the Greek island of Rhodes by the sculptor Chares of Lindos in honor of the isle's patron deity Helios.
DATE / PERIOD: Constructed circa 292–280 BC during the early Hellenistic Period.
DESCRIPTION: The Colossus of Rhodes was a towering bronze statue supported by an iron and stone framework and set near the harbor of the city of Rhodes. Ancient accounts describe a figure roughly 105–110 feet tall, clad in hammered bronze plates over a stone core. Its long-fallen form, described by ancient visitors in precise and measurable detail, remains one of the most influential lost monuments in classical archaeology.
SIGNIFICANCE: The statue commemorated the Rhodians' successful defense against Demetrios Poliorketes and became a pan-Mediterranean emblem of independence. It was counted among the Seven Wonders of the Ancient World and represented a pinnacle of Hellenistic bronze casting and architectural ambition.
WHAT HAPPENED: A major earthquake in 226 BC fractured the statue at the knees and toppled it. Rhodes, following an oracle's instruction, declined to rebuild it. The fallen remains lay on the ground for centuries and were viewed by ancient travelers—until their removal in late antiquity.
PRIMARY SOURCES: Descriptions by Strabo, Pliny the Elder, Philo of Byzantium, Poseidippos of Pella, and later Byzantine chroniclers form the sole surviving ancient testimony.
POSSIBLE SURVIVING FRAGMENTS: No authenticated pieces are known. Ancient writers report that the bronze remnants remained in Rhodes until their reported sale and transport by merchants in the 7th Century AD.
LOCATION LAST KNOWN: The harbor zone of Rhodes, scattered where the statue fell after the 226 BC earthquake.
STATUS: Lost. No verified components have been identified.
REDISCOVERY EFFORTS: Archaeological surveys in and around Mandraki harbor have produced no confirmed structural or bronze elements.
NOTABLE QUOTATIONS ABOUT IT: Pliny the Elder remarked that "few people can clasp the thumb of this statue with both arms," illustrating its immense scale.
LEGACY: The Colossus influenced later monumental statuary and shaped concepts of civic guardianship, living on today as an artistic symbol of Hellenistic ambition.

The Colossus of Rhodes, the gigantic bronze guardian of the city's harbor, half a century before its fall, Rhodes, Greece, circa 280 BC. Illustration copyright © Lochlainn Seabrook.

COMPONENTS OF THE ANTIKYTHERA MECHANISM

TYPE: Lost mechanical components of an ancient Greek bronze astronomical computer.
ORIGIN: Built by Hellenistic engineers skilled in astronomy, mathematics, and precision bronze work, reflecting advanced instrument-making traditions active in the Aegean.
DATE / PERIOD: Circa 150–100 BC, based on paleography and metallurgical studies.
DESCRIPTION: Missing elements include bronze gears, axles, pointers, and inscribed plates that once supported solar, lunar, and eclipse calculations. CT scans show outlines of absent gears and confirm their former integration into coordinated trains essential for differential motion and long-cycle prediction. Several mounting points indicate additional plates or dials that no longer survive.
SIGNIFICANCE: These lost parts limit reconstruction of the mechanism's computational range and remove key evidence for Greek mechanical modeling of long-period astronomical cycles. Their absence obscures one of the most, if not the most, advanced known example of ancient engineering, and constrains efforts to interpret its complete mathematical program.
WHAT HAPPENED: Retrieved in 1901 from a 1st-Century BC shipwreck off the Greek island of Antikythera, the device had endured hundreds of years of corrosion and breakage, causing thin bronze elements to dissolve, fracture, or fuse into concretions. Marine activity further dispersed smaller components.
PRIMARY SOURCES: The surviving fragments, early recovery accounts, and inscriptions preserved on extant plates.
POSSIBLE SURVIVING FRAGMENTS: None confirmed. The missing components likely deteriorated or remain unrecoverable within the wreck's sediment.
LOCATION LAST KNOWN: The Antikythera shipwreck off the island of Antikythera, Greece.
STATUS: Lost, with no additional mechanical pieces recovered.
REDISCOVERY EFFORTS: Later dives with advanced imaging clarified site distribution but revealed no new mechanism parts. Sediment layers continue to inhibit deeper exploration.
NOTABLE QUOTATIONS ABOUT IT: Scholars have described it as "like finding a jet airplane in the tomb of Tutankhamun."
LEGACY: The missing components remain central to interpreting ancient mechanical science and continue to guide reconstructions of Hellenistic astronomical instruments.

Rhodian Greece, 150–100 BC: a craftsman studies the astronomical gearing whose absent segments remain among the mechanism's most significant lost components. Illustration copyright © Lochlainn Seabrook.

CONFEDERATE TREASURE

TYPE: Missing Confederate wartime specie and valuables transported during the 1865 C.S. government retreat.
ORIGIN: Richmond, Virginia.
DATE / PERIOD: April–May 1865.
DESCRIPTION: The treasure consisted of gold and silver coins, bullion, and assorted valuables assembled by the C.S. Treasury as Richmond was evacuated. Exact amounts are uncertain due to incomplete final records. The reserve was escorted by C.S. officials and guards as it moved south by rail and wagon.
SIGNIFICANCE: These funds represented the last financial resources of the Confederate government. Their disappearance influenced postwar claims, local traditions, and long-standing historical interest in the Confederacy's final movements.
WHAT HAPPENED: As Union forces approached Richmond, C.S. officials departed with the available treasury. The hoard passed through Danville, Greensboro, and Charlotte before turning toward Georgia. Portions were issued for payroll and essential expenses as governmental control collapsed. In May 1865, after escorts scattered and civil authority disintegrated, a significant portion vanished amid irregular payments, local seizures, and suspected theft. No conclusive inventory was produced.
PRIMARY SOURCES: Surviving Confederate Treasury correspondence, wartime financial records, Jefferson Davis' papers, eyewitness accounts, military reports, and postwar depositions.
POSSIBLE SURVIVING FRAGMENTS: Small numbers of coins and minor bullion pieces with 1865 provenance survive in private and institutional collections.
LOCATION LAST KNOWN: Southern Georgia in May 1865, particularly the vicinity of Washington, Georgia.
STATUS: Unverified and unrecovered. No authenticated discovery has occurred. (1865 value est. at $1–$3 million in gold and silver.)
REDISCOVERY EFFORTS: Sporadic private searches have taken place since the late 19th Century, relying on memoirs, fragmented documents, and local accounts, without confirmed results.
NOTABLE QUOTATIONS ABOUT IT: Contemporary observers noted the rushed evacuation and poor documentation, contributing to the uncertainty surrounding its fate.
LEGACY: The Lost Confederate Treasure remains a well-known subject in Southern historical study, a tragic reflection of the Confederacy's final days. It continues to attract research interest due to the absence of definitive evidence concerning its fate.

Confederate officer inspecting gold reserves associated with the vanished Confederate Treasury during the government's final retreat into Southern Georgia, April–May 1865. The precious hoard would be worth an estimated $65 million today. Illustration copyright © Lochlainn Seabrook.

COOK EXPEDITION JOURNALS

TYPE: Lost exploration journals from James Cook's Third Voyage.
ORIGIN: Created aboard HMS *Resolution* and HMS *Discovery* by Cook and selected officers during the Pacific expedition, reflecting multiple viewpoints from the crew and scientific personnel.
DATE / PERIOD: 1776–1779.
DESCRIPTION: The officers' journals contained daily entries on landfalls, weather, astronomical measurements, navigation, natural history, and cultural observations. They recorded interactions with Indigenous communities across the Pacific and Arctic, along with ship routines and attempts to locate a northern passage. Each manuscript preserved immediate scientific and geographic data from regions not previously surveyed in detail and documented the expedition's shifting objectives.
SIGNIFICANCE: They provided foundational evidence for Pacific exploration, offering firsthand accounts that shaped later cartography, anthropology, and natural science. Their disappearance removed primary documentation essential for understanding the route, conditions, and decisions of Cook's final voyage, as well as the expedition's broader scientific goals.
WHAT HAPPENED: Multiple journals vanished after Cook's death during Admiralty collection and copying. Some were likely retained privately, misplaced in administrative transitions, or absorbed into uncataloged estates. Others may have been lost during preparation of the 1784 official narrative. No definitive record traces their fate.
PRIMARY SOURCES: Surviving Cook and officer journals in the British Library and National Maritime Museum, 18th-Century Admiralty editions, and correspondence concerning the voyage.
POSSIBLE SURVIVING FRAGMENTS: Notebook leaves, partial copies, and isolated excerpts held in maritime archives and private collections, offering only limited insight into the missing volumes.
LOCATION LAST KNOWN: Admiralty offices in London, England, in the early 1780s.
STATUS: Lost and unrecovered.
REDISCOVERY EFFORTS: Archivists continue examining estate papers, maritime holdings, and uncataloged private materials. Fragments appear but no complete journals.
NOTABLE QUOTATIONS ABOUT IT: Contemporaries praised Cook's journals as "faithful accounts of lands and peoples hitherto unknown," emphasizing their clarity and accuracy.
LEGACY: Their loss has created a lasting gap in Pacific exploration history and limits modern understanding of navigation, cultural contact, and scientific work during Cook's final expedition.

HMS *Resolution* advancing through summer sea ice along the Alaskan coast of the Chukchi Sea, 1778. The missing officers' journals from Cook's Third Voyage have left a gaping hole in our understanding of 18th-Century British naval exploration. Illustration copyright © Lochlainn Seabrook.

CROWN OF THE WELSH PRINCES

TYPE: A medieval regalia ensemble associated with the native rulers of Wales, consisting of a princely crown and related insignia of authority.

ORIGIN: Crafted for the hereditary princes of Gwynedd, the dominant royal house in medieval Wales, whose regalia served as visible confirmation of native rulership.

DATE / PERIOD: Primarily 12th–13th Century, with antecedents rooted in earlier Welsh royal traditions attested in law and chronicle.

DESCRIPTION: A finely worked crown of precious metal accompanied by ceremonial ornaments, known only through textual descriptions and administrative references, with its design reflecting long-standing Insular metallurgical practices.

SIGNIFICANCE: It served as the central emblem of native Welsh authority, representing lawful rule, dynastic legitimacy, and political independence throughout the final phase of native governance.

WHAT HAPPENED: Seized by English forces after the fall of Llywelyn ap Gruffudd in 1282, transported to London as war-booty, entered royal custody, and disappeared from later English treasury lists despite early documentation.

PRIMARY SOURCES: The *Brut y Tywysogion*, English royal financial rolls, and medieval Welsh legal texts concerning princely regalia.

POSSIBLE SURVIVING FRAGMENTS: None known, with no museum or archival holding yielding any authenticated element, and no documented claim emerging from later private collections.

LOCATION LAST KNOWN: In the English royal treasury in the late 13th Century, likely stored alongside other seized regalia from the Welsh campaigns.

STATUS: Lost, with no confirmed record after its transfer to England and no traceable inventory entries in subsequent coronation or treasury documents.

REDISCOVERY EFFORTS: Antiquarian researchers and modern archivists have examined surviving records and regalia catalogues without producing a verifiable lead.

NOTABLE QUOTATIONS ABOUT IT: Chroniclers described its seizure as "the taking of the honor of Wales," emphasizing its symbolic force within the medieval political order.

LEGACY: Its disappearance marked the end of visible native princely sovereignty; it continues to serve as a cultural emblem within Welsh historical memory.

The original hereditary Welsh crown, once part of Wales' princely regalia, has been missing for nearly eight centuries. Illustration copyright © Lochlainn Seabrook.

DEAD SEA SCROLLS

TYPE: The Dead Sea Scrolls comprise a dispersed corpus of early Jewish religious, legal, and communal manuscripts that once formed a unified library. They include biblical books, apocrypha, and sectarian writings of exceptional antiquity.

ORIGIN: Created by Judaean scribes linked to religious communities near the Dead Sea. Their handwriting, language, and materials reflect regional scriptoria devoted to sacred texts.

DATE / PERIOD: Circa 3rd Century BC–1st Century AD, with most copied between circa 150 BC and AD 70.

DESCRIPTION: The cache consisted of parchment and papyrus scrolls stored in caves near Qumran. Contents include biblical manuscripts, commentaries, hymns, and legal and communal material, much of it fragmentary due to age and burial conditions.

SIGNIFICANCE: The scrolls preserve the earliest biblical manuscripts and document diverse Judaean traditions. They provide core evidence for Hebrew textual history and Second Temple religion and remain the primary witness to several variant scriptural traditions.

WHAT HAPPENED: During 1st Century unrest the community hid its library in nearby caves. The scrolls remained unknown until 1947, then were dispersed into various collections.

PRIMARY SOURCES: Surviving manuscripts in authoritative repositories, with supporting archaeological records, early photographs, and accredited scholarly editions.

POSSIBLE SURVIVING FRAGMENTS: Thousands of authenticated pieces remain, including major portions of Isaiah and Deuteronomy, with others likely in private hands.

LOCATION LAST KNOWN: Caves near Qumran, Israel, on the northwest Dead Sea shore, chiefly Caves 1–11, later distributed to institutions in Jerusalem, Amman, and reputable archives.

STATUS: Partially recovered. Unverified by mainstream science regarding further caches, though authenticated fragments continue to emerge.

REDISCOVERY EFFORTS: Continued surveys, excavations, authentication programs, and reconstruction projects aimed at clarifying provenance and reuniting dispersed texts.

NOTABLE QUOTATIONS ABOUT IT: Long regarded as "the greatest manuscript discovery of the 20th Century" for its impact on biblical scholarship.

LEGACY: The scrolls reshaped understanding of early Judaism, anchored study of Hebrew textual development, and remain vital to ancient Near Eastern research.

A 1st Century Judean scribe reviews a newly copied text, part of what would later become known as the now lost Dead Sea Scrolls. Illustration copyright © Lochlainn Seabrook.

DENISOVAN BURIAL TREASURE

TYPE: A presumed cache of symbolic grave goods associated with archaic humans identified as Denisovans. Interpreted as a lost anthropological treasure representing early cultural behavior.

ORIGIN: Southern Siberia, centered on the Altai region. Linked to the Denisovan population known from Denisova Cave and related Pleistocene sites across Central and Eastern Asia.

DATE / PERIOD: Circa 50,000–200,000 years ago. Based on stratigraphy, radiocarbon sampling, and genetic analyses establishing multiple Denisovan occupations.

DESCRIPTION: The treasure refers to inferred mortuary objects once accompanying Denisovan burials. Possible items include bone, ivory, stone, or organic ornaments consistent with symbolic materials in nearby layers; no intact grave has been found yet.

SIGNIFICANCE: A confirmed Denisovan burial with artifacts would redefine early human ritual behavior and provide rare cultural insight into a population known through limited remains and extensive genetic influence. Confirmation would also clarify their relationship to Neanderthals and early modern humans.

WHAT HAPPENED: Any original grave goods were lost through erosion, cave disturbance, climatic cycling, and natural mixing documented in the Altai deposits. Millennia of sediment shifts further obscured original contexts.

PRIMARY SOURCES: Excavation reports from the Siberian Branch of the Russian Academy of Sciences. Peer-reviewed studies detailing Denisovan remains, stratigraphy, and associated cultural material from the Altai.

POSSIBLE SURVIVING FRAGMENTS: Worked bone pieces, pierced teeth, and pendants from relevant layers may reflect Denisovan activity, though none can be confirmed as funerary.

LOCATION LAST KNOWN: Denisova Cave, Altai Mountains, Russia. No verified burial site has yet been identified within the Denisovan range.

STATUS: Lost. No Denisovan funerary assemblage yet recovered.

REDISCOVERY EFFORTS: Continued excavations in Altai caves use sediment DNA, microartifact recovery, and refined stratigraphy to locate undisturbed mortuary contexts.

NOTABLE QUOTATIONS ABOUT IT: Researchers emphasize that burial evidence would significantly expand our understanding of Denisovan cognition and social complexity.

LEGACY: The minimal material record left by this archaic population has left a major gap in early human archaeology, one that could be filled by the discovery of a Denisovan burial trove.

An inferred but yet-to-be-discovered Denisovan burial with wrapped corpse and simple grave goods, Altai Mountains, Russia, circa 50,000–60,000 years ago. Illustration copyright © Lochlainn Seabrook.

DUTCHMAN'S GOLD MINE

TYPE: A legendary lost U.S. gold deposit tied to Southwestern frontier mining traditions. The account emphasizes a hidden lode of unusual richness.

ORIGIN: Rooted in 19th-Century reports attributed to German or German-American prospectors in central Arizona. Later retellings preserved the main storyline.

DATE / PERIOD: Principal versions span the 1840s–1890s based on territorial references. Early 20th-Century publications reinforced the modern form of the narrative.

DESCRIPTION: Said to involve an exceptionally rich vein or cache of native gold concealed in rugged volcanic terrain. Distinct landmarks and narrow access routes appear throughout surviving testimony. Some accounts mention weathered pinnacles and concealed ravines used as reference points.

SIGNIFICANCE: Represents one of the most influential lost-mine traditions in American history, and remains central to Western prospecting folklore and regional identity.

WHAT HAPPENED: Conflicting maps, inconsistent directions, and contradictory witness statements prevented verification. No two preserved accounts align fully.

PRIMARY SOURCES: Territorial newspapers, miner affidavits, Army topographic notes, and early Arizona mining records. Later publications drew directly from these materials.

POSSIBLE SURVIVING FRAGMENTS: No authenticated ore, mining tools, structural remains, or marked features have ever been confirmed.

LOCATION LAST KNOWN: The Superstition Mountains east of modern Phoenix, tied to 19th-Century route landmarks. The region's difficult topography reinforces the persistence of the tradition.

STATUS: Unverified by qualified geologists and historians, with no material evidence supporting any claimed site.

REDISCOVERY EFFORTS: Numerous searches since the early 20th Century have examined ridges, canyons, and mineral-bearing formations. Recent technological surveys renewed interest but revealed no definitive signatures. Modern hobbyist groups occasionally apply updated mapping tools in hopes of clarifying the old trail accounts.

NOTABLE QUOTATIONS ABOUT IT: Territorial-era prospectors called it "a mine of fabulous richness."

LEGACY: Influences American treasure lore, outdoor culture, and regional storytelling, while bolstering frontier mysteries.

Prospector examining a gold-bearing vein associated with the Lost Dutchman's Gold Mine legend in the Superstition Mountains, Arizona Territory, circa 1890. Illustration copyright © Lochlainn Seabrook.

EMERALD TABLET OF HERMES TRISMEGISTUS

TYPE: Esoteric philosophical text attributed to the syncretic Greco-Egyptian sage Hermes Trismegistus, uniting the traditions of Thoth and Hermes.

ORIGIN: Hellenistic Egypt within the Alexandrian hermetic milieu.

DATE / PERIOD: Circulated between the 1st and 3rd Centuries with later preservation in medieval Islamic scholarship.

DESCRIPTION: The Emerald Tablet was a hermetic treatise outlining principles of cosmic order, natural unity, and correspondence between visible and invisible realms. Its compact statements summarized doctrines of generation, transformation, and universal interrelation.

SIGNIFICANCE: The Tablet shaped hermeticism, guided medieval alchemy, and influenced Renaissance natural philosophy. Its doctrine of correspondence informed early scientific thinkers and later esoteric writers, securing its place as a foundational text in Western esotericism.

WHAT HAPPENED: The original artifact disappeared in antiquity, likely lost with the decline of Alexandrian scholarly institutions. The work endured only through Arabic manuscripts and subsequent Latin transmissions.

PRIMARY SOURCES: The earliest known version appears in the Arabic *Kitāb Sirr al-Khalīqa*, attributed to pseudo-Apollonius, with Latin versions circulating by the 12th Century.

POSSIBLE SURVIVING FRAGMENTS: No archaeological fragments or ancient inscriptions exist. All extant forms descend from medieval manuscript tradition.

LOCATION LAST KNOWN: Associated with hermetic circles in Late Antique Egypt, though no precise final location is preserved.

STATUS: Lost as a physical object but partially preserved textually through later witnesses.

REDISCOVERY EFFORTS: Scholars compare Arabic and Latin variants to identify earlier linguistic layers and reconstruct the Tablet's earliest recoverable form.

NOTABLE QUOTATIONS ABOUT IT: Medieval alchemists regarded it as the basis of the transmutational art, and Renaissance thinkers cited it as a concise statement of natural unity.

LEGACY: Its maxim "as above, so below" remains a central hermetic principle and continues to influence esoteric interpretation, symbolic analysis, and metaphysical traditions.

An Egyptian scribe recording a hermetic teaching later linked to the lost original Emerald Tablet of Hermes Trismegistus, circa 3rd Century. Illustration copyright © Lochlainn Seabrook.

ETRUSCAN GOLD BOOKS

TYPE: A group of ancient inscribed gold tablets attributed to the literate elites of pre-Roman Etruria.
ORIGIN: Produced within the cultural sphere of the northern and central Italian Etruscan city-states.
DATE / PERIOD: Traditionally assigned to the 6th–4th Century BC based on paleography and metallurgical comparisons.
DESCRIPTION: These lost gold books consisted of thin gold leaves bound as tablets, engraved with religious, historical, and ritual text in the Etruscan language. Their appearance is partially inferred from comparable Etruscan and Italic gold laminae that preserve script style, ceremonial function, and method of binding. The set likely reflected the formal calligraphy and careful metalworking associated with elite ritual literature.
SIGNIFICANCE: They represented one of the few extended Etruscan written works, offering rare insight into a largely vanished literary tradition. Their contents would have clarified Etruscan theology, law, and linguistic structure, making their disappearance a major loss to classical scholarship.
WHAT HAPPENED: Ancient accounts suggest the tablets were removed from a temple or civic treasury and vanished through conflict, political seizure, or private dispersal. No verified trace appears in later inventories, implying destruction, melting, or unrecorded acquisition.
PRIMARY SOURCES: Classical references, including Varro, mention inscribed Etruscan ritual books. Archaeological parallels such as the Pyrgi gold tablets confirm the medium, format, and ceremonial context.
POSSIBLE SURVIVING FRAGMENTS: No confirmed leaves from the lost set exist, though related ritual laminae offer the closest authenticated comparanda.
LOCATION LAST KNOWN: Within a sanctuary or civic repository of an unidentified Etruscan city.
STATUS: Lost since antiquity with no authenticated sightings.
REDISCOVERY EFFORTS: Scholars examine laminae, sanctuary excavations, and early European collection records for evidence of misattributed fragments.
NOTABLE QUOTATIONS ABOUT IT: Ancient writers emphasized the antiquity and authority of Etruscan ritual books and their role in preserving state rites.
LEGACY: Their loss has deepened the scarcity of Etruscan literature and limited modern understanding of early Italic intellectual culture.

An Etruscan artisan inscribing sacred text onto bound gold books in a scriptorium circa 6th Century BC, part of a ceremonial literary tradition later lost from the historical record. Illustration copyright © Lochlainn Seabrook.

GNOSTIC GOSPELS

TYPE: A dispersed body of early Christian writings attributed to Gnostic teachers and communities whose original Greek gospels survive only in partial form or indirect testimony.

ORIGIN: Produced within Eastern Mediterranean and Near Eastern Christian groups that preserved interpretations of Jesus' teachings centered on inner revelation and spiritual knowledge.

DATE / PERIOD: Composed between the 2nd and 4th Century AD, though some traditions, including elements resembling the Greek Gospel of Thomas, may preserve early 1st-Century Jesuan teachings.

DESCRIPTION: These gospels included dialogues, sayings collections, and revelatory discourses in which Jesus conveyed transformative knowledge. Papyrus codices were copied in monastic and intellectual settings.

SIGNIFICANCE: They formed a notable stream of early Christian literature preserving alternative Christologies and cosmologies. (Note: Over 500 different gospels, many Gnostic, once circulated widely in the early Church.)

WHAT HAPPENED: As institutional Christianity consolidated, many Gnostic writings ceased being copied, fell out of use, or were discouraged and even banned, leading to their disappearance.

PRIMARY SOURCES: Irenaeus, Hippolytus, and Epiphanius quoted or described several lost gospels, preserving fragments while labeling their authors "heterodox" according to emerging doctrinal norms.

POSSIBLE SURVIVING FRAGMENTS: Limited excerpts survive through patristic citations and rare manuscript remnants preserving related sayings or narrative elements.

LOCATION LAST KNOWN: Centers including Alexandria, Syria, Asia Minor, and Egypt, with later presence in monastic libraries.

STATUS: Lost in their original Greek form but partially preserved through later Coptic texts, patristic excerpts, and scattered fragments.

REDISCOVERY EFFORTS: Scholars compare patristic references, extant Gnostic texts, and Egyptian papyri to identify parallels and outline the theology of missing works.

NOTABLE QUOTATIONS ABOUT IT: Irenaeus acknowledged their circulation while asserting they diverged from the doctrines his community upheld.

LEGACY: Their disappearance limits access to early Christian diversity, yet surviving traces remain central to understanding Christianity's formative centuries and its multiple early voices.

A Gnostic teacher preparing Christian codices in an Eastern Mediterranean workshop circa 2nd Century CE, part of a literary tradition later lost to history, Illustration copyright © Lochlainn Seabrook.

GOSPEL OF THE HEBREWS

TYPE: Religious text from the earliest strata of Christian literature; an early Judeo-Christian gospel used by Jewish followers of Jesus.
ORIGIN: Produced within a Jewish-Christian community in the eastern Mediterranean, likely linked to groups preserving Semitic traditions.
DATE / PERIOD: Late 1st to early 2nd Century AD, cited by Church writers into the 4th Century.
DESCRIPTION: A narrative gospel recounting teachings of Jesus for Hebrew-speaking believers, known only through quotations by early Christian authors, displaying Semitic idioms and themes distinct from the canonical Gospels.
SIGNIFICANCE: Demonstrates the diversity of early Christianity and preserves Jewish-Christian interpretations of Jesus.
WHAT HAPPENED: The text declined as Gentile Christianity became dominant, was not copied into later manuscript traditions, and disappeared—except for fragments cited by patristic writers.
PRIMARY SOURCES: Quotations or references appear in the works of Clement of Alexandria, Origen, Jerome, Hegesippus, and Epiphanius.
POSSIBLE SURVIVING FRAGMENTS: Short sayings and narrative excerpts preserved by patristic authors, with no continuous manuscripts or physical leaves surviving.
LOCATION LAST KNOWN: Circulated among Jewish-Christian groups in the Levant and Egypt, last mentioned in late 4th-Century writings.
STATUS: Completely lost apart from patristic quotations preserved in later theological works.
REDISCOVERY EFFORTS: Scholars reconstruct its content through collected quotations, comparative Semitic Gospel studies, and analysis of Jewish-Christian traditions—though no manuscript has emerged from archaeological contexts.
NOTABLE QUOTATIONS ABOUT IT: Jerome described it as "the Gospel which the Nazarenes and Ebionites use" and stated he translated it; Clement of Alexandria cited it for sayings attributed to Jesus.
LEGACY: Remains central to understanding Jewish-Christian communities and the evolution of Gospel traditions, offering a window into Hebrew-oriented expressions of the Jesus movement. Its survival only in later quotations shows how little of the earliest Christian record remains, preserving a narrow glimpse of the Semitic Gospel tradition and how early Jesus-teachings circulated in forms now lost except for echoes in later sources.

Jewish-Christian scribe copying a text connected with the now-lost Gospel of the Hebrews, 1st Century AD. Illustration copyright © Lochlainn Seabrook.

GOSPEL OF THE NAZARENES

TYPE: A Jewish-Christian gospel used by early followers of Jesus who maintained Torah observance and preserved Semitic traditions. It circulated as a written narrative related to Matthew but distinct in wording, structure, and emphasis.

ORIGIN: Composed within Aramaic-speaking Jewish-Christian communities of Judea and Syria. Its theology reflects the beliefs of the Nazarene sect, one of the earliest branches of the Jesus movement and a group noted for adherence to ancestral law and early ritual custom.

DATE / PERIOD: Circa 1st–2nd Century CE, drawing on older Semitic traditions. Patristic references appear between the 3rd and 5th Centuries.

DESCRIPTION: A narrative gospel containing sayings, episodes, halakhic teachings, and Jewish-Christian interpretations of Scripture. Early writers described it as an Aramaic or Hebrew text similar to Matthew but marked by unique readings and alternate legal formulations reflecting Nazarene practice.

SIGNIFICANCE: It preserved an early Semitic witness to Jesus' teachings and offered insight into Jewish-Christian theology and practice. Its loss removed a major source for reconstructing primitive gospel traditions.

WHAT HAPPENED: The text vanished as Nazarene communities declined under Byzantine authority. Only quotations and brief descriptions in later authors survived.

PRIMARY SOURCES: Jerome, Epiphanius, Origen, and Eusebius, whose citations and notices constitute all remaining evidence.

POSSIBLE SURVIVING FRAGMENTS: Patristic excerpts preserving variant readings, brief sayings, and Nazarene interpretations of Matthew.

LOCATION LAST KNOWN: Ecclesiastical archives in Roman Palestine and Syria.

STATUS: Lost since the early medieval period, preserved solely through secondary witnesses.

REDISCOVERY EFFORTS: Scholars examine patristic citations, compare Semitic gospel traditions, and analyze early Hebrew and Aramaic manuscript families for traces of Nazarene material.

NOTABLE QUOTATIONS ABOUT IT: Jerome stated that the Nazarenes possessed a Hebrew gospel "according to the Apostles" and that he consulted it for its antiquity.

LEGACY: It remains central to understanding Jewish-Christian origins and the development of early gospel texts, shaping modern reconstructions of Semitic sources behind the New Testament.

A Nazarene scribe copying an early Hebrew gospel used within the Judean community, a text now known only through later patristic citations, circa 2nd Century CE. Illustration copyright © Lochlainn Seabrook.

HOLY GRAIL

TYPE: A sacred liturgical vessel described in early Christian and medieval European tradition. Considered a relic of exceptional spiritual status. (Note: Some consider it symbolic not literal.)

ORIGIN: Linked to early Christian rites in Roman Judea and later integrated into Western European sacred literature.

DATE / PERIOD: Traditionally placed in the 1st Century AD. Expanded in the 12th–15th Centuries within Latin and vernacular romances.

DESCRIPTION: Commonly identified as a cup or chalice used in early Eucharistic practice. Medieval manuscripts assigned symbolic, royal, mystical, and penitential attributes to it.

SIGNIFICANCE: Influenced European ideas of divine authority and pilgrimage culture. Its literary evolution shaped Western concepts of quest symbolism and spiritual legitimacy.

WHAT HAPPENED: No verified early Christian chalice with Grail associations is documented after Late Antiquity. Medieval writers layered new meanings onto older liturgical themes, obscuring any original referent and merging separate traditions into a unified legend.

PRIMARY SOURCES: The New Testament accounts of the Last Supper (see e.g., Mt. 26:27–28). Early Christian liturgical references. Medieval romances including Chrétien de Troyes' *Perceval* and Robert de Boron's *Joseph d'Arimathie*. Later prose cycles expanded the narrative with additional theological motifs.

POSSIBLE SURVIVING FRAGMENTS: Several medieval chalices have been proposed, but none possess verifiable links to early Christian Jerusalem.

LOCATION LAST KNOWN: No documented historical location. Medieval writers variously placed it in the Near East, Britain, Gaul, or Iberia.

STATUS: Lost. No confirmed artifact survives in any authenticated ecclesiastical treasury.

REDISCOVERY EFFORTS: Pursued by antiquarians, ecclesiastical historians, and explorers since the 19th Century, with searches centered on European sites tied to Grail narratives.

NOTABLE QUOTATIONS ABOUT IT: Chrétien de Troyes described the vessel in ritual procession. Robert de Boron associated it with Joseph of Arimathea and early Christian memory.

LEGACY: Became one of Western civilization's most influential sacred symbols. Continues to shape Christian literature, art, theology, mysticism, and cultural imagination through themes of purity, authority, and the pursuit of esoteric sacred knowledge.

Shortly before it disappears from history, a Judean Christian ponders the sacred vessel long associated with the earliest Jesus communities, circa AD 30. Illustration copyright © Lochlainn Seabrook.

HONJŌ MASAMUNE

TYPE: A Japanese tachi forged by the Kamakura-period master Gorō Nyūdō Masamune. Long regarded as one of the finest blades in Japanese history.
ORIGIN: Sagami Province in eastern Honshu. Produced within the Soshu-den school that defined Masamune's forging style. Created under technical conditions that shaped later metallurgical traditions.
DATE / PERIOD: Late 13th Century. Assigned to Masamune's mature working years. Represents a formative period in the refinement of the Soshu style.
DESCRIPTION: A curved single-edged sword with a complex nie-rich hamon and refined jigane. Praised for exceptional balance, durability, and workmanship. Featured a visually distinctive temper line admired by later appraisers.
SIGNIFICANCE: Served as a Tokugawa symbol of authority. Passed through major daimyo families before becoming the shogunate's principal heirloom. Functioned as a ceremonial representation of political legitimacy.
WHAT HAPPENED: Surrendered during Allied disarmament in 1945 and transferred to a U.S. serviceman through official channels. Its trail ends immediately after this documented handover, marking a major cultural loss in the postwar transition.
PRIMARY SOURCES: Tokugawa inventories listing it as a hereditary treasure. Edo-period documentation confirming shogunal custody; Japanese records from the 1945 confiscation process.
POSSIBLE SURVIVING FRAGMENTS: None known. No verified fittings or blade sections traceable to the Tokugawa piece.
LOCATION LAST KNOWN: Mejiro Police Station, Tokyo, during December 1945 disarmament procedures.
STATUS: Unrecovered. No authenticated sighting has been reported since 1945.
REDISCOVERY EFFORTS: Japanese authorities and sword societies examine archives and markets for unregistered Masamune work, focusing on misattributed Soshu blades.
NOTABLE QUOTATIONS ABOUT IT: Tokugawa sources describe it as a blade of highest merit. Edo appraisers regarded it as a masterwork of classical craftsmanship.
LEGACY: The Honjō Masamune remains Japan's most famous missing sword, representing the cultural losses that accompanied the immediate postwar era. Its absence continues to influence national preservation efforts.

A Kamakura retainer examines the prized but now vanished tachi long associated with Japan's most influential warrior lineage, circa late 13th Century. Illustration copyright © Lochlainn Seabrook.

INCA GOLD OF ATAHUALPA

TYPE: A royal Inca ransom treasure of gold, silver, and ceremonial artworks assembled to secure the release of Sapa Inca Atahualpa from Spanish captivity. It is regarded as the largest documented concentration of imperial Inca precious metalwork.
ORIGIN: Imperial Inca Empire in the central Andes of present-day Peru. Crafted by state metalsmiths in royal workshops in Cuzco and regional centers. Directly associated with Atahualpa, last ruler of a unified Inca realm.
DATE / PERIOD: Circa 1532–1533 during the initial Spanish invasion led by Francisco Pizarro. Events span Atahualpa's capture at Cajamarca through his execution.
DESCRIPTION: The treasure comprised large quantities of ritual gold and silver objects including vessels, plaques, temple fittings, royal emblems, and sculptural works gathered from shrines and palaces across the empire. The ransom was measured by volume, filling a chamber to a marked line.
SIGNIFICANCE: The hoard embodied the political and religious authority of the Inca state. Its destruction removed many of the finest examples of imperial Andean metalwork and marked the rapid decline of indigenous imperial power.
WHAT HAPPENED: Atahualpa ordered regional governors to deliver precious metalwork to Cajamarca in exchange for his freedom. Spanish accounts confirm its immense scale. The treasure was melted into standardized ingots for division among the conquistadors—despite the ransom being met and Atahualpa's execution.
PRIMARY SOURCES: Accounts by Hernando Pizarro, Pedro Pizarro, Miguel de Estete, and Francisco de Xerez.
POSSIBLE SURVIVING FRAGMENTS: None are known. All documented material was melted in the 16th Century.
LOCATION LAST KNOWN: The ransom room at Cajamarca, northern Peru.
STATUS: Lost. No intact objects are known to survive.
REDISCOVERY EFFORTS: Numerous searches for undispatched shipments or concealed caches have produced no authenticated finds.
NOTABLE QUOTATIONS ABOUT IT: Francisco de Xerez wrote that the treasure "surpassed all that had ever been seen" in the Indies.
LEGACY: The loss of Atahualpa's ransom symbolizes the destruction of Inca imperial material culture and remains one of the world's most consequential vanished treasures.

Inca treasure gathered for Atahualpa's 1533 ransom, a royal cache that vanished soon after its assembly. Illustration copyright © Lochlainn Seabrook.

KNIGHTS TEMPLAR TREASURE

TYPE: A consolidated treasury of gold, silver, coinage, reliquaries, manuscripts, and sacred artifacts linked to the Order of the Poor Knights of Christ and of the Temple of Solomon. Included financial reserves, sovereign deposits, and ecclesiastical valuables.

ORIGIN: Formed through donations, royal gifts, battlefield spoils, and banking revenues. Centralized within major European and Levantine commanderies.

DATE / PERIOD: Circa 1119–1312, with peak accumulation in the 12th and 13th Centuries.

DESCRIPTION: A multi-part store of wealth supporting the Order's military, religious, and financial operations. Contemporary references mention sealed chests, relics, documents, and accounts, though no full inventory survives.

SIGNIFICANCE: It reflected the Order's economic strength, international scope, and papal protection. Its loss altered European political dynamics and weakened early continental banking structures. The disappearance influenced later discussions of medieval secrecy and displaced assets.

WHAT HAPPENED: King Philip IV of France arrested the Templars in 1307 and sought their holdings. Confiscated inventories proved partial, with multiple chests and deposits unaccounted for. No verified recovery occurred.

PRIMARY SOURCES: Papal bulls of Innocent II and Clement V, French trial records, royal financial registers of Philip IV, and contemporary chronicles, such as Guillaume de Nangis.

POSSIBLE SURVIVING FRAGMENTS: Scattered documents, seals, and liturgical items preserved in European archives. No authenticated treasure pieces survive.

LOCATION LAST KNOWN: Paris Temple precinct and nearby commanderies at the time of the 1307 arrests, with additional holdings earlier recorded in Cyprus and the Latin East.

STATUS: Unrecovered and unverified.

REDISCOVERY EFFORTS: Investigations of former commanderies, monastic vaults, and archival materials have produced no confirmed results. Research continues to focus on discrepancies in the 1307 seizure documents.

NOTABLE QUOTATIONS ABOUT IT: French records mention "goods and chests not found," and inquisitorial notes reference "treasures removed before arrest."

LEGACY: The disappearance became a defining symbol of the Order's abrupt fall and remains central to studies of medieval finance, state power, and religious-military institutions.

Treasury clerk reviewing a portion of the sealed Templar deposits shortly before their disappearance in 1307. Illustration copyright © Lochlainn Seabrook.

LEAVES OF THE BEOWULF MANUSCRIPT

TYPE: Lost manuscript leaves from an Old English heroic epic.
ORIGIN: Anglo-Saxon England.
DATE / PERIOD: Late 10th to early 11th Century.
DESCRIPTION: These missing folios once belonged to the single surviving Beowulf manuscript, copied by two Anglo-Saxon scribes. They likely contained text lines or marginal material now absent from the poem's physical structure, creating gaps in the codex's original arrangement. Their loss also obscures quire composition and the manuscript's physical sequence.
SIGNIFICANCE: The Beowulf manuscript is the sole source for the poem, giving each missing leaf major textual weight. Their loss removes evidence of Old English vocabulary, orthography, and scribal practice, limiting efforts to reconstruct narrative order and codicological design. The absent leaves also hinder analysis of how the poem was used and preserved in its early life.
WHAT HAPPENED: The 1731 Ashburnham House fire weakened the manuscript's binding and margins, causing later losses through crumbling and handling. Several folios known to early antiquarians no longer survive, and some deteriorated beyond legibility before conservation began.
PRIMARY SOURCES: Humfrey Wanley's catalog entries; Cotton Library stewardship notes; the 1786–1787 transcripts produced for Grímur Jónsson Thorkelin; 19th-Century British Museum conservation records.
POSSIBLE SURVIVING FRAGMENTS: Only charred slivers remain, many mounted on paper frames during Victorian restoration. A few readings survive solely in Thorkelin's pre-fire transcripts.
LOCATION LAST KNOWN: Cotton Library (Ashburnham House), Westminster, London, 1731.
STATUS: Lost. No complete leaves have been recorded since the 19th Century.
REDISCOVERY EFFORTS: Scholars have reviewed private antiquarian holdings and early copies, but no detached folios have been recovered. Modern imaging has clarified surviving leaves without revealing additional material.
NOTABLE QUOTATIONS ABOUT IT: Wanley called the codex "a very ancient book." Thorkelin described it as "almost perished."
LEGACY: The missing leaves demonstrate the fragile transmission of early English literature and shape all modern editions of Beowulf, emphasizing the poem's reliance on a single damaged manuscript.

Anglo-Saxon scribe at work on the now-lost leaves that once formed part of the Beowulf codex, circa AD 1000. Illustration copyright © Lochlainn Seabrook.

LIBRARY OF ALEXANDRIA

TYPE: A state-supported repository of papyrus scrolls and scholarly records central to Hellenistic intellectual life.
ORIGIN: Established by the early Ptolemies in Alexandria, Egypt, as part of a royal program to gather and preserve knowledge.
DATE / PERIOD: Founded circa early 3rd Century BC and active through the Roman Imperial period.
DESCRIPTION: The Library of Alexandria functioned within the Museion as a research institution holding hundreds of thousands of scrolls. Its collections covered literature, science, mathematics, medicine, philosophy, and geography. Scholars produced editions, commentaries, translations, and catalogues, including early bibliographic systems attributed to Callimachus. It served as a working center for long-term textual preservation and comparative research.
SIGNIFICANCE: It became the preeminent center of classical learning, advancing philology, mathematics, astronomy, and textual criticism. Its holdings preserved unique works, authoritative copies, and scholarly commentaries foundational to later intellectual traditions. The institution influenced later Mediterranean educational systems by standardizing texts and critical methods.
WHAT HAPPENED: The Library experienced damage and loss during successive conflicts, including Caesar's Alexandrian War in 48 BC, urban unrest in the 3rd Century AD, and late Roman policies curtailing Pagan institutions. Its collections dispersed or deteriorated across several centuries. (Note: Later tradition falsely framed the Library's decline as a single burning event.)
PRIMARY SOURCES: Testimonies preserved in Strabo, Plutarch, Seneca, Aulus Gellius, Ammianus Marcellinus, Orosius, and later Byzantine compilations.
POSSIBLE SURVIVING FRAGMENTS: No confirmed manuscripts survive, though later copies of classical texts may descend from exemplars once held there.
LOCATION LAST KNOWN: The Brucheion district of ancient Alexandria adjoining the royal quarter.
STATUS: Lost.
REDISCOVERY EFFORTS: Archaeological and underwater surveys of Alexandria's royal and harbor districts continue, but no identifiable remains have been verified.
NOTABLE QUOTATIONS ABOUT IT: Seneca characterized the collection as "a splendid show of the wealth of kings."
LEGACY: The Library stands as a lasting emblem of classical scholarship and the vulnerability of accumulated knowledge.

Scholars gathering at the Library of Alexandria's in the Royal Quarter of ancient Alexandria, Egypt, circa 250 BC. The royal scholarly holdings associated with the Alexandrian Museion formed one of antiquity's largest literary collections, the original scrolls of which completely disappeared over the following centuries. Illustration copyright © Lochlainn Seabrook.

MAYA CODICES

TYPE: A pre-Hispanic corpus of Maya hieroglyphic screenfold manuscripts preserving astronomy, divination, calendrics, and elite scientific knowledge.

ORIGIN: Created by trained scribes of Classic and Postclassic Maya courts throughout southern Mexico, Belize, Guatemala, and western Honduras.

DATE / PERIOD: Circa 9th–16th Century, with conceptual roots in earlier Classic intellectual traditions.

DESCRIPTION: These fig-bark books, coated with lime gesso and painted with black, red, and Maya blue pigments, contained eclipse and Venus tables, deity cycles, rain charts, and ritual almanacs structured through strict numerical patterning.

SIGNIFICANCE: They embodied the highest level of Maya scientific literacy, guiding agriculture, royal ceremony, state ritual, and seasonal observances, and formed the only continuous indigenous literate tradition of the ancient Americas.

WHAT HAPPENED: Most were burned in 16th Century ecclesiastical campaigns, and others perished from humidity, insects, conflict, or decay, leaving only the Dresden, Madrid, Paris, and Grolier manuscripts from a once-large corpus.

PRIMARY SOURCES: The four extant codices, colonial testimonies describing their destruction, indigenous chronicles, and archaeological data on scribal workshops and palace libraries.

POSSIBLE SURVIVING FRAGMENTS: None beyond the four authenticated manuscripts, though murals, ceramics, and carved panels preserve imagery related to lost codical themes.

LOCATION LAST KNOWN: Palatial libraries, priestly schools, and court repositories across Yucatán, Chiapas, Campeche, Quintana Roo, Belize, and Guatemala before Spanish suppression.

STATUS: Lost, unverified by modern scholarship, yet reflected in postcontact Maya calendrical and astronomical continuities.

REDISCOVERY EFFORTS: Investigations of sealed rooms, dry caves, and collapsed palaces continue, while multispectral analyses of the four surviving manuscripts recover structural details of the vanished corpus.

NOTABLE QUOTATIONS ABOUT IT: Chroniclers wrote that Maya books contained "all their sciences," though most were condemned and burned as "superstitions," a loss later seen as culturally devastating.

LEGACY: Their disappearance left major gaps in Maya intellectual history; surviving manuscripts remain central to script decipherment, preserving the last traces of this scientific tradition.

A Maya scribe preparing a folded bark-paper manuscript in a palace workshop, circa AD 1200. This corpus would eventually disappear, the result of burnings, humidity, insects, and decay. Illustration copyright © Lochlainn Seabrook.

MENORAH OF THE SECOND TEMPLE

TYPE: A sacred gold ritual candelabrum central to Temple worship in Jerusalem. Constructed as a seven-branched lampstand of pure hammered gold; served as a perpetual-light symbol within the Holy Place.

ORIGIN: Commissioned according to Mosaic instruction in the Hebrew Bible. Crafted by Israelite artisans following Exodus 25:31–40. Maintained through successive Temple administrations.

DATE / PERIOD: Originally described circa 13th Century BC. Second Temple version active from circa 516 BC until AD 70. Used throughout the Second Temple priestly cycles.

DESCRIPTION: A single shaft with six lateral branches ornamented with almond blossoms, cups, and knobs. Designed to hold seven oil lamps fueled by consecrated olive oil. Weighed one talent of gold (about 75 lbs) according to tradition.

SIGNIFICANCE: Functioned as one of Judaism's most sacred implements. Represented divine presence, cosmic order, and Israel's covenant identity. Appeared in Roman depictions as a key symbol of the Temple.

WHAT HAPPENED: Seized by Roman forces under Titus during the sack of Jerusalem in AD 70. Transported to Rome as war spoils and paraded in the Triumph; deposited in the Temple of Peace treasury.

PRIMARY SOURCES: Hebrew Bible (Exodus, Leviticus, Numbers). Flavius Josephus's *Jewish War*. Tacitus's *Histories*. Arch of Titus relief.

POSSIBLE SURVIVING FRAGMENTS: No authenticated fragments are known. Claimed relics lack verifiable provenance.

LOCATION LAST KNOWN: Temple of Peace, Rome, circa late 1st Century AD. Later movements are undocumented.

STATUS: Lost since antiquity. Unverified by mainstream scholarship, yet traditions maintain a later survival.

REDISCOVERY EFFORTS: Searched for by Jewish scholars, antiquarians, and modern investigators. No confirmed evidence has surfaced.

NOTABLE QUOTATIONS ABOUT IT: Josephus calls it "a candlestick made of gold, of extraordinary weight and workmanship" (Jewish War 7.148). The Arch of Titus presents it as the chief captured object.

LEGACY: Remains one of Judaism's most powerful cultural symbols. Influenced later Jewish art and national iconography. Continues to represent continuity and the lasting historical heritage of the Temple.

Temple priest tending the now lost seven-branched candelabrum during the Second Temple service, circa AD 70. Illustration copyright © Lochlainn Seabrook.

MONTEZUMA'S TREASURE

TYPE: A vast imperial hoard of gold, silver, turquoise mosaics, sacred regalia, and royal tribute belonging to the Aztec Empire.

ORIGIN: Created and assembled within the Triple Alliance domains, centered on Tenochtitlan, under the authority of Emperor Moctezuma II.

DATE / PERIOD: Late Postclassic Period, circa early 16th Century.

DESCRIPTION: Chroniclers describe an immense royal treasury containing precious metals, carved jade, turquoise inlay, featherwork, ritual objects, and war gear. Its core holdings reflected centuries of tribute and ceremonial production overseen by palace workshops, with items crafted for both ritual and administrative purposes.

SIGNIFICANCE: The imperial treasury symbolized divine kingship, state authority, and Aztec economic power and embodied ritual prestige and the fiscal strength that sustained the empire's networks of tribute and alliance.

WHAT HAPPENED: After the Spanish arrival in 1519, portions of the treasure were seized, cataloged, and melted down. During the retreat of 1520, large quantities were lost in canals and causeways, and further holdings vanished during the 1521 siege of Tenochtitlan.

PRIMARY SOURCES: Testimonies by Bernal Díaz del Castillo, Hernán Cortés, and indigenous informants preserved in early colonial codices and chronicles.

POSSIBLE SURVIVING FRAGMENTS: A limited number of mosaics, ornaments, and ritual objects preserved in museum collections with verified pre-Conquest provenance.

LOCATION LAST KNOWN: Palace structures and state repositories within Tenochtitlan, along with segments lost during the retreat toward Tlacopan.

STATUS: Lost, scattered, or destroyed, with only documented artifacts surviving in controlled collections.

REDISCOVERY EFFORTS: Searches have focused on canal beds, former causeways, palace precincts, and rumored burial sites, though no authenticated caches have been recovered.

NOTABLE QUOTATIONS ABOUT IT: Bernal Díaz described seeing "the greatest wealth we had ever beheld." Cortés referred to "treasure beyond estimation."

LEGACY: The lost hoard remains a defining emblem of Aztec sovereignty and a subject of continuing scholarship and cultural memory.

Now vanished imperial valuables at the royal palace treasury of Tenochtitlan, early 16th Century. Illustration copyright © Lochlainn Seabrook.

NAZI GOLD HOARD

TYPE: A dispersed cache of gold bullion, coinage, jewels, and financial assets seized by the Third Reich. Assembled through coercive state appropriation and wartime plunder. Represents one of history's largest accumulations of illicit wealth.

ORIGIN: Collected under the authority of the Reichsbank, SS, and other Nazi agencies during occupations across Europe. Includes valuables taken from governments, banks, and individuals.

DATE / PERIOD: 1933–1945, with peak consolidation from 1939–1945 during World War II.

DESCRIPTION: Composed of thousands of refined gold bars, melted coinage, foreign currency, gemstones, and jewelry. Much of the metal was smelted into uniform bars for transport. Exact quantities remain unknown due to destroyed or incomplete documentation.

SIGNIFICANCE: Provides material evidence of the financial policies and predatory economics of the Third Reich. Influenced postwar restitution law and international debate over stolen assets.

WHAT HAPPENED: As Allied forces advanced in 1945, Nazi officials moved or hid large quantities of gold in mines, tunnels, and Alpine sites. U.S. forces recovered major deposits at Merkers and elsewhere. Additional portions removed by SS units were never located. Postwar investigations traced widespread laundering into global banking systems.

PRIMARY SOURCES: U.S. Army and OSS reports from 1945. U.S. Treasury investigations. Reichsbank records seized by Allied forces. European restitution files.

POSSIBLE SURVIVING FRAGMENTS: Verified Merkers gold survives in national reserves; untraced quantities may persist as integrated bullion within financial circulation.

LOCATION LAST KNOWN: Various evacuation and concealment sites across Germany and Austria, including Thuringian mines and Alpine routes.

STATUS: Unverified by mainstream scholarship, with part recovered and significant portions missing.

REDISCOVERY EFFORTS: Allied recovery missions from 1945–1950. Later governmental audits. Periodic modern archival reassessments of wartime transfers.

NOTABLE QUOTATIONS ABOUT IT: "The greatest treasure find in history." — U.S. Army report, 1945.

LEGACY: Continues to inform research on wartime looting, restitution policy, and the long-term impact of Nazi economic crimes.

Late-war German personnel documenting bullion transfers linked to the wartime hoard, most of which vanished without a trace after 1945. Illustration copyright © Lochlainn Seabrook.

NIBELUNGEN HOARD

TYPE: A legendary royal treasure of the historical Germanic Burgundians, preserved in medieval Germanic heroic tradition and long associated with the Nibelung cycle.
ORIGIN: Burgundian royal wealth tied to the court at Worms, later connected in narrative form to Attila's domains during the migration period.
DATE / PERIOD: Linked to circa 5th-Century Burgundian events; recorded in 12th–13th Century manuscripts that preserve earlier oral material.
DESCRIPTION: A substantial assemblage of bullion, jewelry, and worked metal described as requiring multiple wagons for transport and functioning as a major dynastic asset. Medieval sources emphasize its role as a symbol of Burgundian authority.
SIGNIFICANCE: The hoard illustrates the scale of Burgundian royal wealth and later shaped Germanic epic literature, influencing themes of inheritance, loyalty, and political conflict. Its enduring presence in heroic tradition reflects how early medieval societies preserved historical memory.
WHAT HAPPENED: Medieval accounts state that the treasure passed from Siegfried to the Burgundians, later through Kriemhild, and was ultimately concealed near the Rhine by Hagen. The tradition holds that the hiding place was never disclosed and that the treasure vanished from the historical record.
PRIMARY SOURCES: *Nibelungenlied*; *Þiðreks saga*; *Völsunga saga*; related Germanic and Norse chronicles referencing Burgundian tradition.
POSSIBLE SURVIVING FRAGMENTS: None authenticated; reported river finds remain unverified and cannot be linked to the hoard with certainty.
LOCATION LAST KNOWN: A concealed site along the Middle Rhine associated with Burgundian narrative geography.
STATUS: Lost. No credible documentation supports any claim of rediscovery, and no archaeological work has produced evidence.
REDISCOVERY EFFORTS: From the 19th Century onward, antiquarians and local searchers examined riverbank sites and manuscript clues without yielding results, though interest remains active.
NOTABLE QUOTATIONS ABOUT IT: Medieval tradition held that the treasure was so vast "that thirty wagons could not bear it."
LEGACY: The hoard endures as a cornerstone of Germanic legend and remains central to discussions of Burgundian heritage, heroic narrative, and migration-era cultural memory.

Fifth-Century Burgundian custodian overseeing the royal hoard during its final movements along the Rhine River before it passed into legend. Illustration copyright © Lochlainn Seabrook.

NORSE GREENLAND MONASTIC LIBRARY

TYPE: Episcopal library of the Norse Greenland Church containing liturgical, theological, legal, and administrative manuscripts. Served as the colony's principal intellectual and ecclesiastical archive.

ORIGIN: Founded at Gardar after 1124 with the establishment of the Greenland diocese. Developed under bishops trained in Norway and Iceland and supported by shipments from Scandinavia.

DATE / PERIOD: 12th–15th Century. Active from Bishop Arnald's consecration to the final abandonment of the settlements. Represented the height of organized Christian administration in Norse Greenland.

DESCRIPTION: Held Latin parchment codices such as missals, breviaries, homiliaries, canon law texts, and diocesan registers. Stored within the bishop's residence adjacent to Gardar Cathedral and maintained by trained clergy.

SIGNIFICANCE: Documented sacraments, land rights, tithes, correspondence, and governance. Demonstrated Norse Greenland's participation in European literacy and medieval Church administration.

WHAT HAPPENED: The collapse of the Norse settlements led to the desertion of Gardar. Loss of clergy, the close of shipping, and structural decay resulted in the disappearance of all manuscripts.

PRIMARY SOURCES: Papal letters concerning the Greenland bishopric. Icelandic annals noting episcopal appointments. Norwegian ecclesiastical correspondence. Archaeological studies of the Gardar complex.

POSSIBLE SURVIVING FRAGMENTS: None identified. Any remnants were likely destroyed by climate, reuse, or dispersal during abandonment.

LOCATION LAST KNOWN: Episcopal residence and cathedral precinct at Gardar, Eastern Settlement, near present-day Igaliku, Greenland.

STATUS: Lost. No codex, register, or fragment from the monastic library is known to survive.

REDISCOVERY EFFORTS: Excavations at Igaliku since the 19th Century have documented buildings but no manuscripts. Continued survey work targets buried structural remnants.

NOTABLE QUOTATIONS ABOUT IT: Contemporaneous Ecclesiastical letters describe Greenland as remote yet fully integrated into Christendom.

LEGACY: Represents the vanished written record of an Arctic diocese and a rare example of high medieval Christian literacy in the far North.

The episcopal complex at Gardar, Greenland, during the late 13th Century, where the now lost diocesan library was housed. Illustration copyright © Lochlainn Seabrook.

NORSE SAGAS

TYPE: Medieval Scandinavian prose narratives forming Iceland's foundational literary corpus, including family sagas, kings' sagas, and legendary sagas. Many were later copied into vellum manuscripts.
ORIGIN: Iceland and Norway.
DATE / PERIOD: Circa 1100–1400.
DESCRIPTION: These prose texts preserved ancestral memory, early settlement history, royal lineages, and exploration traditions. They combined oral transmission with clerical literacy. Many original exemplars disappeared, leaving only later copies derived from missing archetypes and occasional unique manuscript clusters.
SIGNIFICANCE: The sagas are the central written record of medieval Scandinavian society and contain the earliest accounts of Iceland, Greenland, Vinland, and pre-Christian Norse culture. Their lost forms remain vital for reconstructing vanished historical and literary material and for tracking the development of Northern prose traditions.
WHAT HAPPENED: Early manuscripts were lost through decay, fire, damp, and institutional transitions. Many sagas survive only in incomplete redactions, fragments, or references to now-missing texts recorded by later scribes.
PRIMARY SOURCES: Surviving vellum manuscripts such as *Hauksbók*, *Möðruvallabók*, *Flateyjarbók*, *Codex Regius*, and *AM* volumes. Icelandic annals and clerical inventories record additional lost works.
POSSIBLE SURVIVING FRAGMENTS: Partial leaves, isolated chapters, and excerpted passages preserved in later compilations or quoted within other medieval texts.
LOCATION LAST KNOWN: Ecclesiastical scriptoria, monastic libraries, and private farm collections in medieval Iceland and Norway.
STATUS: Lost or incomplete, with partial survivals permitting limited reconstruction.
REDISCOVERY EFFORTS: Manuscript cataloging, paleography, and comparative textual study by Icelandic and international scholars.
NOTABLE QUOTATIONS ABOUT IT: Icelandic scholars have described the saga tradition as the "inheritance of a nation."
LEGACY: These lost sagas shaped the study of medieval Scandinavia, informed modern literature, and remain essential to understanding Norse identity, early North Atlantic history, and the evolution of written storytelling in the North.

A 13th-Century Icelandic scribe contributing to the textual transmission underlying the lost Norse Sagas. Illustration copyright © Lochlainn Seabrook.

ORIGINAL NEW TESTAMENT

TYPE: The original handwritten autographs of the 27 canonical New Testament books composed by the earliest Christian authors. These manuscripts once existed as individual scrolls and codices written in 1st-Century Koine Greek. No confirmed examples are known to survive. Today's NT books all derive from later copies.

ORIGIN: Eastern Mediterranean regions associated with the earliest Christian communities, including Judea, Syria, Asia Minor, and Greece. Church tradition assigns authorship to the Apostles, but modern scholarship regards the original writers as uncertain.

DATE / PERIOD: Approximately AD 45–100, representing the earliest generation of Christian literary activity.

DESCRIPTION: The autographs were ink-on-papyrus manuscripts produced by their authors or trained scribes. Each circulated independently before later compilation into broader collections, forming the earliest written foundation of the Christian movement.

SIGNIFICANCE: These manuscripts constitute the foundational textual witnesses to early Christianity. They supply the earliest documentary record of apostolic teaching. Because the autographs no longer exist, the exact original wording of the New Testament cannot be known with absolute certainty, and all modern texts rely on later manuscript traditions.

WHAT HAPPENED: Fragile papyrus, continuous use, and repeated copying led to natural deterioration. Environmental conditions and historical upheavals hastened their disappearance.

PRIMARY SOURCES: Patristic quotations preserved by Clement of Rome, Ignatius of Antioch, Irenaeus of Lyons, Tertullian, Origen, and Eusebius. Early manuscript families and lectionaries provide indirect evidence.

POSSIBLE SURVIVING FRAGMENTS: No authenticated fragments exist, though later papyri preserve early text forms.

LOCATION LAST KNOWN: Various early Christian centers across the eastern Roman Empire.

STATUS: Lost to history with no verified remnants.

REDISCOVERY EFFORTS: Scholars analyze ancient papyri, patristic citations, and textual lineages to approximate original readings.

NOTABLE QUOTATIONS ABOUT IT: Origen noted variations among manuscripts, indicating awareness that the earliest copies were no longer available.

LEGACY: Their disappearance shaped New Testament textual criticism, introduced errors into later reconstructions, and influenced the transmission of Christian doctrine and literature.

An early Christian messenger carrying several now lost 1st-Century scrolls, part of what we would consider to have been part of the original New Testament. (Note: Currently the Codex Sinaiticus, from the 4th Century, is our oldest *complete* copy of the New Testament.) Illustration copyright © Lochlainn Seabrook.

PALLADIUM OF TROY

TYPE: A sacred protective image associated with divine guardianship, traditionally described as a small wooden statue of the multifaceted state goddess, Pallas Athena.

ORIGIN: Rooted in Bronze Age Anatolian religion and incorporated into Homeric and Classical Greek tradition as Troy's central cult object.

DATE / PERIOD: Referenced in Late Bronze Age mythic cycles and preserved in early Greek epic poetry and later Classical historiography.

DESCRIPTION: A carved wooden figure of Athena holding a spear and shield, regarded as a divine pledge of Troy's security. Classical authors describe it as ancient, severe in style, and tied to early pre-Hellenic ritual forms.

SIGNIFICANCE: The Palladium (literally, a "sacred image of Pallas Athena") symbolized Troy's divine sanction and was believed to ensure the city's inviolability. Greek and Roman writers treated possession of the relic as a source of political and religious authority, influencing later ideas of sacred state protection.

WHAT HAPPENED: Tradition maintains that Odysseus and Diomedes secretly removed the Palladium during the Trojan War, weakening Troy's protection and contributing to its fall. Later accounts place it in Greek sanctuaries and ultimately in Rome's Temple of Vesta, where it was venerated as a national safeguard.

PRIMARY SOURCES: Homeric hymnic material, the Epic Cycle, Apollodorus, Dionysius of Halicarnassus, Livy, and Roman antiquarian writers.

POSSIBLE SURVIVING FRAGMENTS: No authenticated fragments exist. Later "Palladia" in Greek and Roman shrines represent ritual copies rather than parts of the original, created to perpetuate its protective symbolism.

LOCATION LAST KNOWN: Roman tradition situates it within the Temple of Vesta in the Forum under care of the Vestal Virgins.

STATUS: Lost to history with no verifiable archaeological trace.

REDISCOVERY EFFORTS: Excavations in the Roman Forum and studies of the Vestal complex have yielded no artifact identifiable as the Palladium.

NOTABLE QUOTATIONS ABOUT IT: Dionysius of Halicarnassus called it "the safeguard of the city" preserved in Vesta's temple.

LEGACY: The Palladium influenced later concepts of state-protecting relics and contributed to ongoing symbolism linking divine favor to civic security.

The Palladium, guardian symbol of Troy and later preserved in Rome's sacred hearth tradition, ensconced within the Vestal sanctuary under the charge of the Vestal Virgins, circa 12th Century BC. Illustration copyright © Lochlainn Seabrook.

PLAYS OF SHAKESPEARE

TYPE: Lost literary manuscripts consisting of the original authorial drafts of the plays traditionally attributed to Shakespeare.
ORIGIN: Conventionally ascribed to William Shakespeare of Stratford-upon-Avon.
DATE / PERIOD: Late 16th Century to early 17th Century.
DESCRIPTION: A corpus of roughly three dozen plays whose original manuscripts, working drafts, and holographs have never been located. Surviving texts derive from later printings based on theatrical copies, scribal reconstructions, or promptbooks. The absence of any verified holograph prevents direct study of the author's handwriting, revisions, and working method.
SIGNIFICANCE: These manuscripts would clarify original wording, authorial revisions, staging intentions, textual variants, and patterns of collaboration. Their recovery would provide definitive evidence for compositional methods and theatrical practice.
WHAT HAPPENED: No evidence confirms the survival of Shakespeare's original working papers after his lifetime. Early printers relied on non-authorial manuscripts, reflecting the performance-centered document culture of early modern theater. Their absence has sustained authorship debates involving Sir Francis Bacon, Christopher Marlowe, and Edward de Vere, among others.
PRIMARY SOURCES: Early quartos, the 1623 First Folio, theatrical records, legal documents, and references by Elizabethan and Jacobean writers.
POSSIBLE SURVIVING FRAGMENTS: No verified holograph pages exist; a few annotated volumes have been proposed but remain unproven.
LOCATION LAST KNOWN: Uncertain, likely within theatrical companies, scribal collections, or London printing houses.
STATUS: Lost. Their disappearance preserves open debate concerning textual origins, authorial identity, and early modern transmission.
REDISCOVERY EFFORTS: Searches in English archives, private collections, and institutional holdings have yielded no authenticated manuscripts.
NOTABLE QUOTATIONS ABOUT IT: Ben Jonson praised the author's "well turned and true-filed lines," underscoring the value of the vanished originals.
LEGACY: Their loss required reconstruction from secondary sources and ensured a central role for editorial scholarship in defining the Shakespearean canon.

A Jacobean noblewoman preserving a circulating but now vanished manuscript linked to the Shakespearean plays, circa 1605-1620. Illustration copyright © Lochlainn Seabrook.

POEMS OF SAPPHO

TYPE: A corpus of lyric poetry by the archaic Greek poet Sappho of Lesbos.

ORIGIN: Island of Lesbos in the northeastern Aegean, within the cultural sphere of Archaic Greece.

DATE / PERIOD: Circa 630–570 BC, preserved in antiquity in a standardized nine-book Alexandrian edition.

DESCRIPTION: The Poems of Sappho comprised hymns, epithalamia, love lyrics, devotional pieces, and personal reflections written in Aeolic Greek. Only modest fragments survive, most quoted by later authors or recovered from papyri. Note: Nothing in the surviving record suggests that Sappho departed from the customary heterosexual norms of women in archaic Greek society.

SIGNIFICANCE: Sappho's corpus formed one of the foundational bodies of Greek lyric and shaped classical aesthetics and later Hellenistic scholarship. Her work influenced major Roman poets, who cited her for emotional precision and technical mastery. Later critics regarded her imagery as a model of refined lyric craft.

WHAT HAPPENED: The nine-book edition gradually disappeared between Late Antiquity and the Middle Ages as Greek literary culture contracted. Transmission diminished due to selective copying priorities and limited medieval demand for secular Pagan lyric.

PRIMARY SOURCES: Quotations and testimony in Dionysius of Halicarnassus, Longinus, Athenaeus, Hephaestion, Hermogenes, and later Byzantine lexica.

POSSIBLE SURVIVING FRAGMENTS: Papyrus pieces from Oxyrhynchus and other Egyptian sites; the Cologne papyri; fragments in ancient treatises; the *Tithonus Poem*; the *Brothers Poem*; and the *Hymn to Aphrodite*.

LOCATION LAST KNOWN: Hellenistic and Roman libraries in Alexandria, Pergamon, and other centers of textual scholarship with later traces in Byzantine compilations.

STATUS: Unverified by modern scholarship but known through authenticated ancient quotations and papyri.

REDISCOVERY EFFORTS: Papyrological excavation in Egypt and philological reconstruction by classical scholars. Renewed analysis of older holdings continues to yield additional word-recoveries.

NOTABLE QUOTATIONS ABOUT IT: Longinus praised Sappho's ability to evoke "the irresistible onrush of emotion" and cited her as a standard of sublime expression.

LEGACY: The lost corpus shaped Western lyric traditions and provided templates for later love poetry.

Sappho studying one of her now-lost papyrus lyrics, Lesbos, Greece, circa 600 BC. Illustration copyright © Lochlainn Seabrook.

POLYNESIAN NAVIGATIONAL TABLETS

TYPE: Instructional mnemonic tablets used by Polynesian and Micronesian master navigators to encode star paths, wave patterns, seabird routes, and landfall indicators.
ORIGIN: Central and Eastern Polynesia with strong preservation in the Caroline Islands, linked to hereditary navigator guilds.
DATE / PERIOD: Pre-contact origins extending into late prehistory, with forms present into the 17th–18th Centuries.
DESCRIPTION: Compact wooden or fiber tablets incised or cord-bound to store symbolic cues for long-distance wayfinding. Lines conveyed swell direction, star risings, currents, and relational positions of island groups. They served strictly as teaching devices, not onboard tools.
SIGNIFICANCE: They embodied a refined empirical science of non-instrument navigation that enabled long-distance Pacific voyaging. Their structure demonstrates the observational precision and cultural continuity of indigenous oceanic knowledge systems.
WHAT HAPPENED: Navigator schools restricted access, limiting transmission. Missionary suppression, colonial pressure, warfare, and cultural change caused their disappearance. By the late 19th Century observers reported the original instructional tablets lost.
PRIMARY SOURCES: Ethnographic interviews with surviving master navigators; early field notes by Pacific scholars documenting pre-missionary wayfinding traditions; oral testimony describing tablet functions.
POSSIBLE SURVIVING FRAGMENTS: A few disputed or partial specimens in museums, none confirmed as complete pre-contact tablets.
LOCATION LAST KNOWN: Various islands across Polynesia and Micronesia where navigator guilds maintained hereditary training houses.
STATUS: Lost. No authenticated, intact navigational tablet is known to survive.
REDISCOVERY EFFORTS: Scholars and wayfinding practitioners have compared oral accounts with rare museum pieces; but none has produced a verified original tablet.
NOTABLE QUOTATIONS ABOUT IT: Early researchers described them as "mnemonic charts of the sea" capturing the "invisible geometry" of Pacific navigation.
LEGACY: While their loss demonstrates the fragility of indigenous scientific systems, their memory has fueled the modern renaissance of Polynesian wayfinding and the reconstruction of ancestral navigation.

A Polynesian woman studying a now vanished traditional navigational tablet in preparation for an open-ocean voyage, circa 1750. Illustration copyright © Lochlainn Seabrook.

REGALIA OF CHARLEMAGNE

TYPE: Coronation regalia associated with the Carolingian imperial office.

ORIGIN: Frankish Empire, likely created in workshops connected to Aachen, Germany, and surrounding ecclesiastical centers.

DATE / PERIOD: Circa 8th–9th Century.

DESCRIPTION: The Regalia of Charlemagne consisted of ceremonial objects used for imperial consecration, including a crown, lance, sword, sceptre, orb, and supporting liturgical items. These pieces embodied Christian authority, dynastic legitimacy, and the sanctified transfer of rulership within the Carolingian state.

SIGNIFICANCE: The regalia formed the ritual core of Western imperial coronations and became primary symbols of Carolingian legitimacy. Their association with Charlemagne elevated them to one of Europe's most venerated assemblages of sacred and political authority.

WHAT HAPPENED: Across the medieval and early modern eras the corpus dispersed through war, plunder, replacement, and dynastic transition. Several early pieces were destroyed or melted, while later replicas entered ceremonial use as originals vanished. Turmoil during the Reformation, the Thirty Years' War, and the Napoleonic period erased clear provenance.

PRIMARY SOURCES: Einhard's *Vita Karoli Magni*, the *Royal Frankish Annals*, imperial inventories, Aachen treasury records, and liturgical ordines describing coronation procedure.

POSSIBLE SURVIVING FRAGMENTS: Elements within medieval regalia preserved in Vienna show early workmanship, though none can be confirmed as Carolingian originals based on surviving documentation.

LOCATION LAST KNOWN: Imperial treasuries and strongholds linked to Aachen and later Holy Roman ceremonial centers.

STATUS: Lost, with components destroyed, altered, or absorbed into later regalia without verifiable lineage.

REDISCOVERY EFFORTS: Scholarship relies on archival reconstruction, textual comparison, and technical examination of medieval regalia in light of Carolingian liturgical practice.

NOTABLE QUOTATIONS ABOUT IT: Medieval commentators described the regalia as consecrated instruments of divine kingship and imperial continuity.

LEGACY: The lost assemblage shaped coronation practice for centuries and remains central to understanding Carolingian rulership, medieval political theology, and the evolution of European imperial symbolism.

A Carolingian attendant inspecting Charlemagne's now lost imperial regalia in the treasury chamber, circa 800-900. Illustration copyright © Lochlainn Seabrook.

ROMAN LEGION IX SCROLLS

TYPE: A lost corpus of Roman military documents believed to contain operational records, dispatches, and intelligence reports from Legio IX Hispana ("the Ninth Spanish Legion").

ORIGIN: Produced by Roman officers attached to the Ninth Legion, likely compiled in Britannia during the early Imperial period.

DATE / PERIOD: Circa 1st–2nd Century AD, during the legion's final attested decades.

DESCRIPTION: The Roman Legion IX Scrolls denote a presumed set of administrative records—rosters, supply tallies, campaign notes, construction logs, and correspondence—maintained on papyrus or parchment within the legion's archive chest.

SIGNIFICANCE: The scrolls may have preserved decisive information on the legion's disappearance, offering rare insight into Roman military organization, deployment, and provincial governance in northern Britannia.

WHAT HAPPENED: The legion vanishes from the Roman record after the early 2nd Century AD, and its archive disappears with it, likely through destruction during frontier unrest, loss during redeployment, or routine deterioration.

PRIMARY SOURCES: Tacitus, Cassius Dio, Roman military diplomas, imperial inscriptions, and parallels from surviving legionary archives.

POSSIBLE SURVIVING FRAGMENTS: No authenticated fragments exist; only scattered inscriptions referencing Legio IX Hispana survive, none derived from its archival records.

LOCATION LAST KNOWN: The legion's headquarters at Eboracum (modern York, England) or a temporary northern frontier installation in Roman Britannia.

STATUS: Lost; unverified by modern scholarship, with the probability of survival considered extremely low.

REDISCOVERY EFFORTS: Archaeological surveys and excavations at forts across northern England and southern Scotland have refined the legion's footprint but revealed no archival materials.

NOTABLE QUOTATIONS ABOUT IT: Modern scholars describe the legion's archival absence as "one of the most vexing gaps in the Roman military record."

LEGACY: The lost scrolls epitomize the fragility of ancient Rome's documentary tradition and continue to influence studies of imperial administration, frontier warfare, and the unresolved fate of Legio IX Hispana.

Ancient Roman courier delivering the now vanished Legio IX scrolls, circa AD 108–120. Illustration copyright © Lochlainn Seabrook.

ROMANOV CROWN JEWELS

TYPE: Regalia, crown jewels, and ceremonial gemstones of the Russian Imperial family.
ORIGIN: Commissioned by Romanov rulers using Russian, European, and Asian gem sources.
DATE / PERIOD: 17th–early 20th Century.
DESCRIPTION: The Romanov Crown Jewels included the Imperial Crown, scepters, orbs, diadems, necklaces, brooches, and curated loose diamonds for state ceremony. Many pieces featured historic stones such as the Orlov and Shah diamonds and displayed the highest levels of Russian and European craftsmanship.
SIGNIFICANCE: The regalia symbolized dynastic legitimacy, imperial authority, and the wealth of the Russian Empire. They served as ceremonial anchors during coronations, diplomatic events, and state portraiture, reinforcing the public image of an unbroken royal lineage.
WHAT HAPPENED: After the 1917 Revolution, the Bolsheviks seized the jewels. Some were cataloged and photographed, while others were dismantled or sold during state auctions in the 1920s–1930s. Several pieces disappeared during early Soviet transfers, internal handling, or foreign sales.
PRIMARY SOURCES: The 1922 Soviet "Catalogue of Crown Jewels," Russian coronation records, treasury inventories, gemological examinations, and authenticated auction documentation.
POSSIBLE SURVIVING FRAGMENTS: Individual stones believed to originate from dismantled items occasionally surface in archives or private collections, though full provenance is rare.
LOCATION LAST KNOWN: Soviet repositories in Moscow, chiefly the Armory Chamber and Gokhran, during the early 20th Century.
STATUS: Partially extant, with numerous components missing or absorbed into untraceable collections.
REDISCOVERY EFFORTS: Archival researchers and gem specialists continue to review early Soviet lists, foreign auction records, and private collection histories for evidence of dispersed items.
NOTABLE QUOTATIONS ABOUT IT: Soviet officials in 1922 called the jewels "a unique artistic and historical inheritance of the former empire."
LEGACY: The missing Romanov jewels embody the collapse of an imperial dynasty and remain a case study in the vulnerability of state regalia during political transition.

Russian imperial court attendant with the Romanov family jewels, including the Great Imperial Crown, scepter, and orb, Winter Palace, Russia, circa 1905. Illustration copyright © Lochlainn Seabrook.

SCROLL OF PYTHEAS OF MASSALIA

TYPE: A lost scientific travel manuscript by the Greek explorer Pytheas of Massalia, composed after his voyage to the far North.
ORIGIN: Written in Massalia (modern Marseille, France) by Pytheas, a 4th Century BC navigator, astronomer, and geographer.
DATE / PERIOD: Circa 4th Century BC, following his exploratory journey around the North Atlantic.
DESCRIPTION: Known in antiquity as *On the Ocean*, the scroll recorded Pytheas's observations of the Atlantic, the British Isles, the Arctic Circle, tidal rhythms, and northern peoples. It included early accounts of Thule, sea ice, polar seasons, astronomical measurements, and northern ethnography.
SIGNIFICANCE: It was the earliest detailed Greek eyewitness report of northern Europe and the first known scientific account of the Arctic regions. It introduced the Mediterranean world to high-latitude geography and the relationship between lunar cycles and tides.
WHAT HAPPENED: The scroll disappeared in antiquity, likely lost during the transmit-and-copy process that ended many early Greek scientific works. No complete manuscript survived into the major medieval copying centers, and by the Roman period it was already considered irretrievable.
PRIMARY SOURCES: Quotations and paraphrases from Pytheas's lost work survive in fragments preserved by Strabo, Pliny the Elder, Diodorus Siculus, Polybius, and Geminus.
POSSIBLE SURVIVING FRAGMENTS: No physical manuscript remains; scattered textual extracts embedded in later classical authors represent the only surviving material.
LOCATION LAST KNOWN: Classical Mediterranean scholarly circles, likely in Massalia or in the libraries of early Greek geographers.
STATUS: Lost in antiquity with no known manuscript copies, though its content survives indirectly through fragmentary quotations.
REDISCOVERY EFFORTS: Classical philologists continue to reconstruct portions of the scroll through comparative analysis of ancient citations, but no direct text has been recovered.
NOTABLE QUOTATIONS ABOUT IT: Strabo doubted Pytheas's claims but preserved key passages, while Pliny the Elder cited him as an authority on northern geography.
LEGACY: This lost scroll shaped ancient and modern understandings of northern exploration and established Pytheas as the earliest scientific voyager of the Atlantic.

Pytheas navigating the northern British coast along the route described in his now-lost 4th-Century BC account. Illustration copyright © Lochlainn Seabrook.

SECRET GOSPEL OF MARK

TYPE: A lost esoteric Christian gospel attributed to Mark, known only through a letter ascribed to Clement of Alexandria (to Theodore) describing an expanded edition of the canonical text.
ORIGIN: Early Christian community in Alexandria, linked to the Markan tradition and reserved for advanced (that is, mystical) instruction according to Clement.
DATE / PERIOD: Circa 1st–2nd Century AD for the gospel, with the Clement letter dated to the late 2nd Century AD.
DESCRIPTION: A longer but "secret" or spiritually elite version of the Gospel of Mark containing additional teachings and a resurrection account involving a young man. The text is preserved solely in two excerpts copied into an 18th-Century printed book.
SIGNIFICANCE: One of the most important missing documents of early Christianity. It suggests multiple Markan editions and offers insight into Alexandrian theology and tiered catechesis within early Christian communities. The work provides rare evidence for controlled textual traditions that circulated outside the public liturgical sphere.
WHAT HAPPENED: The expanded gospel fell out of circulation as Christian scripture standardized. The only known witness was the Clement letter found at Mar Saba in 1958. The manuscript was later removed and has not been recovered.
PRIMARY SOURCES: The letter attributed to Clement of Alexandria addressed to Theodore and preserved through photographs taken in 1958.
POSSIBLE SURVIVING FRAGMENTS: Two quoted passages embedded in the Clement letter. No independent manuscript has survived, but it is supported by the NT (see e.g., Mt. 13:10–11).
LOCATION LAST KNOWN: Margins of a 17th-Century printed volume at Mar Saba Monastery near Jerusalem.
STATUS: Lost, with the physical letter pages missing, with authenticity disputed but no separate copy of the gospel known.
REDISCOVERY EFFORTS: Searches of monastic libraries in Palestine and Egypt and scholarly comparisons within Alexandrian textual studies.
NOTABLE QUOTATIONS ABOUT IT: Clement describes the material as "more spiritual," intended for those "being perfected."
LEGACY: The fragments illustrate early Christian textual diversity and match broader patterns of vanished apostolic writings, including Paul's reference to an earlier missing letter (1 Corinthians 5:9). The work remains central to studies of Markan development, Alexandrian thought, and mystical Christianity.

Jesus instructing a select circle of spiritually elite students in the Judean hills, sharing advanced esoteric knowledge later said to have been recorded in the purported Secret Gospel of Mark. Numerous New Testament passages speak plainly of Jesus' esoteric teaching methods, an enigmatic *gnosis*, an arcanum of "secrets" and "mysteries," that He reserved for a special class of His more spiritually evolved followers. See e.g., Matthew 13:10-11, 34-36; 24:3; Mark 4:10-12; Luke 8:9-10; John 16:12. Illustration copyright © Lochlainn Seabrook.

SIBYLLINE BOOKS

TYPE: Prophetic religious texts revered in the ancient Mediterranean world and consulted by Roman authorities during crises.

ORIGIN: Composed in Greek by an early oracular tradition attributed to a legendary prophetic female figure known as the Sibyl—later maintained in Rome as the *Libri Sibyllini*.

DATE / PERIOD: Created circa 6th Century BC, preserved in various curated redactions through the late Roman Empire.

DESCRIPTION: A collection of oracular verses offering ritual and political guidance during prodigies, disasters, and military emergencies. The books blended archaic Greek hexameters with Near Eastern prophetic elements and were accessed only by the *quindecimviri sacris faciundis*. Their consultation required formal authorization from the Senate, reflecting the strict legal and religious controls surrounding their use.

SIGNIFICANCE: The books influenced Roman statecraft for centuries and shaped the official response to omens, public rites, foreign cult introductions, and periods of instability. Their authority linked divine sanction with civic policy.

WHAT HAPPENED: The original Capitoline set was destroyed in the fire of 83 BC. A replacement corpus was assembled from oracular texts gathered across the Mediterranean and placed under official review. These later books disappeared during the 5th Century AD, likely destroyed amid Christian efforts to eliminate Pagan archives.

PRIMARY SOURCES: Cited or described by Dionysius of Halicarnassus, Livy, Varro, Tacitus, Suetonius, Lactantius, and Zosimus.

POSSIBLE SURVIVING FRAGMENTS: Later Sibylline Oracles contain echoes of archaic material but are heavily reworked and cannot be matched with certainty to the Roman state collection.

LOCATION LAST KNOWN: Temple of Apollo Palatinus, Rome.

STATUS: Lost.

REDISCOVERY EFFORTS: Philologists and historians have analyzed linguistic strata within oracular literature in hopes of isolating original verses, but no authenticated passages have emerged.

NOTABLE QUOTATIONS ABOUT IT: Described by Dionysius of Halicarnassus as providing "divine sanction" for Rome.

LEGACY: The books shaped Roman religious authority and influenced later Jewish and Christian apocalyptic literature, remaining a defining symbol of state-directed prophecy in antiquity.

A Roman state priest consulting the now-lost prophetic texts once safeguarded by Roman authorities, circa 1st Century AD. Illustration copyright © Lochlainn Seabrook.

SUMERIAN KING LISTS

TYPE: A corpus of early Mesopotamian royal registers written in cuneiform. Documents listing rulers, reign lengths, and dynastic succession across Sumer.

ORIGIN: Compiled by Sumerian scribes in southern Mesopotamia. Produced in temple and palace scriptoria and transmitted through administrative archives.

DATE / PERIOD: Earliest versions circa 3rd Millennium BC. Standardized form circulating by the early 2nd Millennium BC. Used and copied into the 1st Millennium BC.

DESCRIPTION: The lists traced a sequence from antediluvian rulers to historical dynasties in cities such as Kish, Ur, and Isin. Each entry named the king, his city, and his reign length. Mythic reigns appeared beside historically credible records, reflecting tradition and political aims.

SIGNIFICANCE: The lists shaped early Mesopotamian chronology and codified the doctrine that kingship "descended from heaven." They preserved political memory, offered dynastic legitimacy, and provided a model for later royal historiography.

WHAT HAPPENED: The original recension disappeared through archive destruction, loss, and political turnovers. Later copies varied in completeness, order, and scribal interpretation.

PRIMARY SOURCES: Old Babylonian and Middle Babylonian clay tablets preserving partial versions. Fragments recovered at Nippur, Larsa, and related sites, supplemented by later scribal citations.

POSSIBLE SURVIVING FRAGMENTS: Several incomplete tablets held in museum collections. No surviving exemplar preserves the full archetype, though overlaps allow partial reconstruction.

LOCATION LAST KNOWN: Palace and temple archives of major Sumerian and early Babylonian cities. Exact repository of the master copy is unknown.

STATUS: Lost in its complete form. Preserved only in variant manuscript fragments and traditions.

REDISCOVERY EFFORTS: Archaeological expeditions since the 19th Century have uncovered fragments. Philologists continue comparing variants to approach the earliest recoverable text.

NOTABLE QUOTATIONS ABOUT IT: Opens with the formula "After kingship descended from heaven, kingship was in Eridu," encapsulating Sumerian royal theology.

LEGACY: The lists influenced later Mesopotamian king lists and supported the development of chronological science, as well as helping formulate ancient Near Eastern concepts of political continuity and historical order.

A temple scribe recording royal succession in a Mesopotamian archive now lost to history, circa 2nd Millennium BC. Illustration copyright © Lochlainn Seabrook.

TEMPLAR FLEET

TYPE: A dispersed maritime treasure fleet linked to the Knights Templar's financial, liturgical, and administrative assets. Comprised of vessels capable of transporting gold, documents, relics, and portable wealth.

ORIGIN: Organized under Templar authority in Atlantic ports such as La Rochelle, France, during the order's suppression and drawing on its established maritime network.

DATE / PERIOD: Circa 1307–1308 during the arrests ordered by King Philip IV and the dissolution overseen by Pope Clement V.

DESCRIPTION: A small convoy believed to have removed treasury reserves, sacred objects, and selected records before confiscation. Surviving testimonies reference stored cargo, sudden departures, and missing inventories.

SIGNIFICANCE: Represents the last movement of confirmed Templar assets and is central to the unresolved disappearance of the order's movable wealth and archives. Its loss affects modern studies of medieval banking and military logistics.

WHAT HAPPENED: On the night of October 12–13, 1307, Templar ships reportedly sailed from La Rochelle before royal officers arrived. Their destinations were concealed, and no vessel was officially recorded again.

PRIMARY SOURCES: Early 14th Century arrest records, inquisitorial transcripts, papal correspondence, royal fiscal registers, and chronicles referencing the La Rochelle departures.

POSSIBLE SURVIVING FRAGMENTS: No authenticated cargo, archival material, or hull remains directly linked to the fleet have been recovered.

LOCATION LAST KNOWN: The harbor of La Rochelle on France's Atlantic coast during the initial wave of arrests in October 1307.

STATUS: Lost. No confirmed archaeological, archival, or material trace has surfaced.

REDISCOVERY EFFORTS: Archival work in French and Iberian repositories and maritime surveys in the Bay of Biscay have produced no verified results.

NOTABLE QUOTATIONS ABOUT IT: One French chronicler remarked that the ships "slipped away before the king's men appeared."

LEGACY: The vanished fleet remains central to Templar studies, shaping interpretations of the order's final logistics. Its disappearance continues to influence research into medieval finance, maritime mobility, and the end of the Templar institution.

The outbound Templar convoy, loaded with the order's treasures, as it appeared in 1307—now vanished from the pages of history. Illustration copyright © Lochlainn Seabrook.

TOMB OF CLEOPATRA VII AND MARK ANTONY

TYPE: A royal burial complex constructed for Cleopatra VII Philopator and Mark Antony, the final rulers of Ptolemaic Egypt. Its form reflected late Hellenistic–Egyptian funerary architecture.
ORIGIN: Commissioned in Alexandria by Cleopatra VII and completed under Roman supervision after her death.
DATE / PERIOD: Late 1st Century BC during the final years of the Ptolemaic state and the rise of Roman authority.
DESCRIPTION: Ancient writers describe a joint tomb containing their embalmed bodies, royal ornaments, and items tied to their reign. Its layout and decoration remain unknown, though it likely combined Egyptian and Greek elements typical of elite Alexandrian burials.
SIGNIFICANCE: The burial represented the political and personal union of Egypt's last monarchs and marked the symbolic end of independent pharaonic rule.
WHAT HAPPENED: The tomb persisted into the early Roman Imperial era, but centuries of earthquakes, shoreline collapse, and urban renewal obscured or destroyed its setting. No ancient record describes its final fate.
PRIMARY SOURCES: Plutarch's *Life of Antony*; Cassius Dio's *Roman History*; Strabo's *Geography*; Suetonius's *Life of Augustus*.
POSSIBLE SURVIVING FRAGMENTS: No confirmed fragments survive, and no identified Ptolemaic components have been linked to Cleopatra or Antony.
LOCATION LAST KNOWN: Somewhere in ancient Alexandria, likely within or adjacent to the palace quarter near the eastern harbor.
STATUS: Lost. Its location, design, and contents remain undiscovered.
REDISCOVERY EFFORTS: Archaeological investigations in Alexandria's urban core and underwater districts have targeted the Ptolemaic royal zone since the 19th Century. Research at Taposiris Magna and Marina el-Alamein continues to examine funerary remains using remote sensing and stratigraphic excavation.
NOTABLE QUOTATIONS ABOUT IT: Plutarch records Octavian's command that Cleopatra be buried beside Antony with royal honor.
LEGACY: The missing tomb has become a defining symbol of the dynasty's end and continues to guide modern archaeological interest in Alexandria's vanished palatial district.

Temple attendants preparing royal treasures before the twin sarcophagi of Cleopatra VII and Mark Antony inside their now vanished tomb complex, 30 BC. Illustration copyright © Lochlainn Seabrook.

TOMB OF GENGHIS KHAN

TYPE: The unlocated burial site and accompanying grave goods of the Mongol Empire's founding ruler, traditionally believed to contain elite weapons, ornaments, and ceremonial regalia from the early 13th Century.

ORIGIN: Mongol Empire, Eastern Steppe regions of modern Mongolia.

DATE / PERIOD: Circa early 13th Century, traditionally 1227.

DESCRIPTION: The tomb is described in historical sources as a hidden royal burial in an unmarked location. It likely held personal arms, horse gear, precious metals, and ritual items associated with imperial authority. No architectural or material evidence has ever been identified.

SIGNIFICANCE: As the resting place of one of world history's most consequential figures, the tomb represents a major missing chapter in Eurasian history. Its recovery would illuminate Mongol funerary practice, imperial craftsmanship, and the political culture of steppe rulership.

WHAT HAPPENED: Sources describe a deliberate effort to conceal the site to prevent disturbance, robbery, or political misuse. Accounts mention secrecy by the burial escort, but specifics vary and no archaeological confirmation exists.

PRIMARY SOURCES: *The Secret History of the Mongols*, Rashid al-Din's *Jāmiʿ al-Tawārīkh*, and related 13th–14th Century Persian and Chinese chronicles on imperial burials.

POSSIBLE SURVIVING FRAGMENTS: No authenticated objects, structural elements, or artifacts from the tomb have been recovered.

LOCATION LAST KNOWN: Traditionally associated with the heavily forested Khentii Mountains in northeastern Mongolia—though no verifiable documentation fixes a precise site.

STATUS: Unlocated. No credible archaeological trace has been found.

REDISCOVERY EFFORTS: Limited surveys, remote-sensing projects, and culturally restricted expeditions have examined the region, but Mongolian law and heritage protections limit intrusive work.

NOTABLE QUOTATIONS ABOUT IT: Rashid al-Din noted that Genghis Khan was buried "in the utmost secrecy," underscoring the empire's determination to protect his grave.

LEGACY: The hidden tomb remains one of archaeology's most enduring absences, symbolizing the cultural weight of Mongolian heritage and the unresolved mysteries of early imperial Eurasia.

Forest hollow with hidden earthen entrance to the now lost tomb of Genghis Khan, Khentii Mountains, Mongolia, 13th Century. Illustration copyright © Lochlainn Seabrook.

TREASURE OF LIMA

TYPE: A large colonial bullion cache of gold, silver, jewels, liturgical objects, and royal valuables removed from Lima, Peru, during political unrest.
ORIGIN: Drawn from ecclesiastical treasuries, civic repositories, major estates, and royal holdings in the Viceroyalty of Peru.
DATE / PERIOD: 1820–1821, during the Peruvian War of Independence.
DESCRIPTION: The treasure comprised church ornaments, precious-metal bars, minted coins, reliquaries, and ceremonial vessels. Contemporary inventories report several tons of bullion and valuables, reflecting centuries of Spanish extraction. Its composition mirrors the wealth accumulated by Lima's churches and the administrative capital of Spanish South America.
SIGNIFICANCE: The Lima Treasure represents one of the largest documented transfers of colonial wealth during Latin America's independence struggles, and illustrates the material scale of Spain's imperial presence in Peru. The event also encapsulates the economic dislocation that accompanied the fall of Spanish authority along the Pacific coast.
WHAT HAPPENED: Spanish officials sent the treasure seaward to prevent its capture. Captain William Thompson of the *Mary Dear* was contracted to transport it. Surviving testimony states that Thompson and his crew killed the guards, seized the cargo, and concealed it at Cocos Island, Costa Rica, before their capture. Thompson escaped, and the cache vanished.
PRIMARY SOURCES: Nineteenth-Century maritime records, Spanish colonial correspondence, independence-era testimony, and early Cocos Island expedition accounts held in Peruvian and Spanish archives.
POSSIBLE SURVIVING FRAGMENTS: None authenticated.
LOCATION LAST KNOWN: Aboard the *Mary Dear* near Cocos Island in the eastern Pacific.
STATUS: Lost.
REDISCOVERY EFFORTS: Government and private expeditions have searched Cocos Island since the late 19th Century using excavations, grid mapping, and remote-sensing surveys without confirmed findings.
NOTABLE QUOTATIONS ABOUT IT: Early Peruvian sources referred to it as "the wealth of an empire in flight."
LEGACY: The Treasure of Lima remains a central case of vanished colonial bullion and a major focus of maritime investigation, influencing Pacific exploration and modern treasure-hunting lore.

The 19th-Century British merchant ship *Mary Dear* approaches Cocos Island, Costa Rica, carrying the magnificent but now lost Treasure of Lima, circa 1821. Illustration copyright © Lochlainn Seabrook.

The End

BIBLIOGRAPHY
and Suggested Reading

Aalto, Sirpa. *The Rise of the Mongol Empire: Studies in the Biography of Chinggis Khan*. Tampere, Finland: University of Tampere Press, 2010.
Aland, Kurt, and Barbara Aland. *The Text of the New Testament: An Introduction to the Critical Editions and to the Theory and Practice of Modern Textual Criticism*. Grand Rapids, MI: William B. Eerdmans Publishing Company, 1987.
Albright, William Foxwell. *Archaeology and the Religion of Israel*. Baltimore, MD: Johns Hopkins Press, 1942.
Allen, James P. *The Ancient Egyptian Pyramid Texts*. Atlanta, GA: Society of Biblical Literature, 2005.
Ammianus Marcellinus. *The Later Roman Empire*. Walter Hamilton, trans. Harmondsworth, UK: Penguin Books, 1986.
Anderson, George K. *The Saga of the Volsungs: The Norse Epic of Sigurd the Dragon Slayer*. New York: Columbia University Press, 1936.
Andersson, Theodore M. *The Growth of the Medieval Icelandic Sagas (1180–1280)*. Ithaca, NY: Cornell University Press, 2006.
Apollodorus. *The Library of Greek Mythology*. London, UK: Penguin Classics, 1997.
Aristides. *The Orations of Aristides*. Charles A. Behr, trans. Leiden, Netherlands: Brill, 1981.
Aronson, Theo. *The Golden Bees: The Story of the Amber Room*. London, UK: James Barrie Books, 1966.
Assmann, Jan. *Cultural Memory and Early Civilization: Writing, Remembrance, and Political Imagination*. Cambridge, UK: Cambridge University Press, 2011.
Athenaios. *The Deipnosophists*. Charles Burton Gulick, trans. London, UK: William Heinemann, 1927.
Attridge, Harold W., ed. *The Coptic Gnostic Library: A Complete Edition of the Nag Hammadi Codices*. Leiden, Netherlands: Brill, 2009.
Aulus Gellius. *The Attic Nights*. John C. Rolfe, trans. London, UK: William Heinemann, 1927.
Bacon, Francis. *The Works of Francis Bacon*. London, UK: Longmans, 1857.
Bagehot, Walter. *Lombard Street: A Description of the Money Market*. London, UK: Henry S. King, 1873.
Bagnall, Roger. *Alexandria: Library of Dreams*. Berkeley, CA: University of California Press, 2023.
Baker, G. P. *Tiberius Caesar*. New York: Cooper Square Publishers, 1961.
Ballard, Michael B. *The Confederate Treasury and Treasury Agents, 1861–1865*. Jackson, MS: University Press of Mississippi, 1980.
Barber, Malcolm. *The Trial of the Templars*. Cambridge, UK: Cambridge University Press, 1978.
Barnes, Jay. *The Story of the Lost Dutchman Gold Mine*. Phoenix, AZ: Arizona Historical Foundation, 1970.
Bauer, Walter. *Orthodoxy and Heresy in Earliest Christianity*. Philadelphia, PA: Fortress Press, 1971.
Baur, Ferdinand Christian. *Paul the Apostle of Jesus Christ: His Life and Work, His Epistles and His Doctrine*. London, UK: Williams and Norgate, 1875.
———. *The Church History of the First Three Centuries*. London, UK: Williams and Norgate, 1878.
Baus, Heinrich. *Die Bernsteinzimmer der Könige*. Berlin, Germany: Reimer, 1910.
Beaglehole, J. C., ed. *The Journals of Captain James Cook on His Voyages of Discovery, Volume 3: The Voyage of the Resolution and Discovery*. Cambridge, UK: Hakluyt Society, 1967.

Bennett, Alexander. *Bushido and the Art of the Samurai*. Tokyo: Japan Publishing Industry Foundation for Culture, 2017.
Berdan, Frances F. *Aztec Imperial Strategies*. Washington, D.C.: Dumbarton Oaks, 1996.
Bergk, Theodor. *Poetae Lyrici Graeci*. Leipzig, Germany: B. G. Teubner, 1878.
Best, Lloyd. *The Book of Kells: A Masterwork of Irish Art*. New York: Thames and Hudson, 1999.
Beyer, Hermann. *The Dresden Codex*. Washington, D.C.: Carnegie Institution of Washington, 1921.
Bierhorst, John, trans. *The Codex Chimalpopoca: The Text in Nahuatl with a Glossary and Grammatical Notes*. Tucson, AZ: University of Arizona Press, 1992.
Bingham, Hiram. *A Residence of Twenty-One Years in the Sandwich Islands*. Hartford, CT: Hezekiah Huntington, 1847.
Birley, Anthony R. *The Fasti of Roman Britain*. Oxford, UK: Oxford University Press, 1981.
Birley, Anthony R. *The Roman Government of Britain*. Oxford, UK: Oxford University Press, 2005.
Bjarnarson, Guðni Jónsson, ed. *Völsunga Saga*. Reykjavik, Iceland: Íslendingasagnaútgáfan, 1906.
Boase, T. S. R. *Kingdoms and Strongholds of the Crusaders*. London, UK: Thames and Hudson, 1971.
Bollaert, William. *Antiquarian, Ethnological and Other Researches in New Granada, Equador, Peru and Chile*. London, UK: Trübner and Company, 1860.
Bonfante, Giuliano and Larissa Bonfante. *The Etruscan Language: An Introduction*. Manchester, UK: Manchester University Press, 2002.
Boone, Elizabeth Hill. *Stories in Red and Black: Pictorial Histories of the Aztecs and Mixtecs*. Austin, TX: University of Texas Press, 2000.
Boron, Robert de. *Joseph d'Arimathie: Roman en vers du XIIIe siècle*. Paris: Librairie Renouard, 1874.
Bottéro, Jean. *Mesopotamia: Writing, Reasoning, and the Gods*. Chicago, IL: University of Chicago Press, 1992.
Boutell, Charles. *Monumental Brasses and Slabs*. London, UK: George Bell and Sons, 1847.
Bower, Tom. *Nazi Gold: The Full Story of the Fifty-Year Swiss-Nazi Conspiracy*. New York: HarperCollins, 1997.
Bowra, C. M. *Greek Lyric Poetry: From Alcman to Simonides*. Oxford, UK: Clarendon Press, 1961.
Boyle, J. A., trans. *The Successors of Genghis Khan*. New York: Columbia University Press, 1971.
Brasseur de Bourbourg, Charles Étienne. *Manuscrit Troano: Études sur le Système Graphique et la Langue des Mayas*. Paris: Maisonneuve, 1869.
Bright, John. *A History of Israel*. Philadelphia, PA: Westminster Press, 1959.
Briquel, Dominique. *The Etruscans: History and Civilization*. Bloomington, IN: Indiana University Press, 2015.
Bromley, Allan. *The Antikythera Mechanism: The Story of the World's Oldest Computer*. Sydney, NSW: University of Sydney Press, 2001.
Brooks, Francis. *The Spanish Conquest and the Aztec Empire*. London, UK: Kegan Paul, 1904.
Brown, Raymond E. *The Birth of the Messiah: A Commentary on the Infancy Narratives in the Gospels of Matthew and Luke*. New York: Doubleday, 1977.
Brown, Raymond E. *The Gospel According to John I–XII*. New York: Doubleday, 1966.
Brown, Nancy Marie. *The Far Traveler: Voyages of a Viking Woman*. Orlando, FL: Harcourt, 2007.
Browne, James W. *The Nibelungenlied: Translation and Commentary*. London, UK: Trübner and Company, 1886.
Bruce, F. F. *The Canon of Scripture*. Downers Grove, IL: InterVarsity Press, 1988.
Brueckner, Alexander. *Bernstein und Bernsteinzimmer in Preussen*. Königsberg, Germany:

Hartung, 1896.
Budge, E. A. Wallis. *The Book of the Dead: The Papyrus of Ani*. London, UK: Kegan Paul, 1895.
—. *Egyptian Magic*. London, UK: Kegan Paul, 1899.
Bunbury, Edward Herbert. *A History of Ancient Geography Among the Greeks and Romans*. London, UK: John Murray, 1879.
Bunyakovsky, Gleb. *Archæological Researches in the Altai Mountains*. St. Petersburg, Russia: Imperial Academy of Sciences, 1897.
Burch, George. *The Holy Grail: Its Legends and Symbolism*. London, UK: Thomas Burleigh, 1902.
Burgtorf, Jochen. *The Central Convent of Hospitallers and Templars: History, Organization, and Personnel (1099–1310)*. Leiden, Netherlands: Brill, 2008.
Burkitt, F. C. *Textual Criticism and the Gospel History*. London, UK: Cambridge University Press, 1901.
Burrows, Millar. *The Dead Sea Scrolls*. New York: Viking Press, 1955.
Campbell, Duncan B. *The Fate of the Ninth*. Glasgow, Scotland: Bocca della Verità Publishing, 2018.
Campbell, David A., trans. *Greek Lyric I: Sappho and Alcaeus*. Cambridge, MA: Harvard University Press, 1982.
Canfora, Luciano. *The Vanished Library: A Wonder of the Ancient World*. Berkeley, CA: University of California Press, 1990.
Carlyle, Thomas. *History of Friedrich II of Prussia, Called Frederick the Great*. London, UK: Chapman and Hall, 1858.
Cassius Dio. *Roman History*. Earnest Cary, trans. Cambridge, MA: Harvard University Press, 1914.
Chambers, E. K. *William Shakespeare: A Study of Facts and Problems*. Oxford, UK: Clarendon Press, 1930.
Chambers, William. *The Book of Days: A Miscellany of Popular Antiquities*. London, UK: W. and R. Chambers, 1863.
Chambers, R. W. *Beowulf: An Introduction to the Study of the Poem with a Discussion of the Stories of Offa and Finn*. Cambridge, UK: Cambridge University Press, 1921.
Chiba, Takanori. *The Japanese Sword: A Comprehensive Guide*. Tokyo: Seibundo Shinkosha, 1935.
Chrétien de Troyes. *Le Roman de Perceval ou le Conte du Graal*. Paris: Librairie Firmin-Didot, 1866.
Cicero, Marcus Tullius. *De Divinatione*. William Armistead Falconer, trans. Cambridge, MA: Harvard University Press, 1923.
Cieza de León, Pedro de. *The Discovery and Conquest of Peru*. Alexandra Parma Cook, trans., Noble David Cook, ed. Durham, NC: Duke University Press, 1998.
Clark, Kenneth W. *A Descriptive Catalogue of Greek New Testament Manuscripts in America*. Chicago, IL: University of Chicago Press, 1937.
Cleaves, Francis Woodman, trans. *The Secret History of the Mongols*. Cambridge, MA: Harvard University Press, 1982.
Clement of Alexandria. *The Stromata, or Miscellanies*. Henry K. Plummer, trans. Edinburgh, Scotland: T&T Clark, 1884.
—. *The Exhortation to the Greeks; The Rich Man's Salvation; To the Newly Baptized*. G. W. Butterworth, trans. Cambridge, MA: Harvard University Press, 1919.
Clermont-Ganneau, Charles. *Archæological Researches in Palestine*. London, UK: Palestine Exploration Fund, 1899.
Clunies Ross, Margaret. *The Cambridge Introduction to the Old Norse-Icelandic Saga*. Cambridge, UK: Cambridge University Press, 2010.
Coe, Michael D. *The Maya*. New York: Thames and Hudson, 1966.
Coe, Michael D., and Justin Kerr. *The Art of the Maya Scribe*. New York: Thames and Hudson, 1998.
Collingwood, R. G., and R. P. Wright. *The Roman Inscriptions of Britain, Volume I: Inscriptions on Stone*. Oxford, UK: Clarendon Press, 1965.

Collins, John Churton. *Studies in Shakespeare*. London, UK: Archibald Constable, 1904.
Colonna, Giovanni. *Sacred Writing and Ritual in Etruria*. Rome, Italy: Accademia Nazionale dei Lincei, 1996.
Cook, Stanley Arthur. *The Religion of Ancient Palestine in the Second Millennium B.C.* London, UK: Cambridge University Press, 1908.
Cook, James. *The Journals of Captain James Cook on His Voyages of Discovery*. London, UK: Hakluyt Society, 1893.
Cook, James. *The Voyage of the Resolution and Discovery, 1776–1780*. John C. Beaglehole, ed. Cambridge, UK: Hakluyt Society, 1967.
Cortés, Hernán. *Cartas de Relación*. Madrid, Spain: Imprenta de la Real Academia de la Historia, 1866.
Couch, Arthur J. *The Mechanical Arts of the Ancient Greeks: Studies in Classical Engineering*. London, UK: Longmans, Green, 1899.
Cox, Edward William. *The Annals of the Crusades*. London, UK: William Tegg, 1859.
Craige, William. *The Icelandic Sagas*. London, UK: T. Fisher Unwin, 1901.
Creighton, J. *Coins and Power in Iron Age Britain*. Cambridge, UK: Cambridge University Press, 2000.
Cristofani, Mauro, ed. *The Etruscans: A New Investigation*. London, UK: Thames and Hudson, 1979.
Cunliffe, Barry. *The Extraordinary Voyage of Pytheas the Greek*. London, UK: Allen Lane, 2001.
—. *On the Ocean: The Mediterranean and the Atlantic from Prehistory to AD 1500*. Oxford, UK: Oxford University Press, 2017.
D'Altroy, Terence N. *The Incas*. Cambridge, UK: Cambridge University Press, 2002.
Dalman, Gustaf. *Aramaic Grammar*. Leipzig, Germany: Hinrichs, 1894.
Dalman, Gustav. *The Words of Jesus: Considered in the Light of Post-Biblical Jewish Writings and the Aramaic Language*. Edinburgh, Scotland: T. and T. Clark, 1902.
Davenport, Cyril. *Royal English Bookbindings*. London, UK: Seeley and Company, 1896.
Davies, John. *A History of Wales*. London, UK: Penguin Books, 1993.
Davis, Jefferson. *The Papers of Jefferson Davis, Volume 12: 1865*. Lynda Lasswell Crist and Mary Elizabeth Ellison, eds. Baton Rouge, LA: Louisiana State University Press, 1990.
Davis, William C. *An Honorable Defeat: The Last Days of the Confederate Government*. New York: Harcourt, 2001.
Dawson, Christopher, ed. *Mission to Asia*. New York: Sheed & Ward, 1955.
De Grummond, Nancy Thomson. *Etruscan Myth, Sacred History, and Legend*. Philadelphia, PA: University of Pennsylvania Museum of Archaeology and Anthropology, 2006.
De Rossi, Giovanni Battista. *Roma Sotterranea*. London, UK: Longmans, Green, and Company, 1869.
Delaville Le Roulx, Joseph. *Les Hospitaliers en Terre Sainte et à Chypre, 1100–1310*. Paris, France: Ernest Leroux, 1904.
Derevianko, Anatoly P. *The Paleolithic of Siberia*. Novosibirsk, Russia: Siberian Branch of the Russian Academy of Sciences Press, 1998.
Díaz del Castillo, Bernal. *The True History of the Conquest of New Spain*. London, UK: Hakluyt Society, 1908.
Diehl, Ernst. *Anthologia Lyrica Graeca*. Leipzig, Germany: B. G. Teubner, 1922.
Dillmann, August. *Ethiopic Biblical and Patristic Literature*. London, UK: Williams and Norgate, 1890.
Diodorus Siculus. *The Library of History*. London, UK: Henry G. Bohn, 1843.
Diogenes Laertius. *Lives of Eminent Philosophers*. R. D. Hicks, trans. London, UK: William Heinemann, 1925.
Dionysius of Halicarnassus. *Roman Antiquities*. Earnest Cary, trans. Cambridge, MA: Harvard University Press, 1937.
Dobbie, Elliott Van Kirk, ed. *The Anglo-Saxon Poetic Records, Vol. 4: Beowulf and Judith*. New York: Columbia University Press, 1953.
Dobson, Brian. *The Army of the Roman Republic: The Second Century BC, Polybius and the*

Camps at Numantia, Spain. Oxford, UK: Oxbow Books, 2008.
Domaszewski, Alfred von. *Die Rangordnung des Römischen Heeres*. Vienna, Austria: Alfred Hölder, 1908.
Dorner, Isaac August. *History of Protestant Theology*. Edinburgh, Scotland: T. and T. Clark, 1871.
Dover Wilson, John. *The Manuscript of Shakespeare's Plays: The State of the Text in the Light of Scholarly Research*. Cambridge, UK: Cambridge University Press, 1935.
Doyle, Arthur Conan. *Through the Magic Door*. London, UK: Smith, Elder and Co., 1907.
—. *Memories and Adventures*. London, UK: Hodder and Stoughton, 1924.
Drachmann, A. G. *The Mechanical Technology of Greek and Roman Antiquity: A Study of the Literary Sources*. Madison, WI: University of Wisconsin Press, 1963.
Driver, Samuel Rolles. *An Introduction to the Literature of the Old Testament*. New York: Charles Scribner's Sons, 1891.
—. *An Introduction to the Literature of the Old Testament*. Edinburgh, Scotland: T. & T. Clark, 1897.
Dugdale, William. *Monasticon Anglicanum*. London, UK: Longman, Hurst, Rees, Orme, and Brown, 1817.
Durán, Diego. *The History of the Indies of New Spain*. Norman, OK: University of Oklahoma Press, 1994.
Dutt, Sukumar. *Buddhist Monks and Monasteries of India: Their History and Contribution to Indian Culture*. London, UK: George Allen and Unwin, 1962.
Edersheim, Alfred. *The Temple: Its Ministry and Services as They Were at the Time of Jesus Christ*. London, UK: The Religious Tract Society, 1874.
Edmonds, J. M., trans. *Lyra Graeca: Being the Remains of All the Greek Lyric Poets from Eumelus to Timotheus*. London, UK: William Heinemann, 1922.
Edwards, James R. *The Hebrew Gospel and the Development of the Synoptic Tradition*. Grand Rapids, MI: Eerdmans, 2009.
Ehrman, Bart D. *Lost Scriptures: Books That Did Not Make It into the New Testament*. New York: Oxford University Press, 2003.
Einarsson, Stefán. *A History of Icelandic Literature*. Baltimore, MD: Johns Hopkins Press, 1957.
El-Abbadi, Mostafa. *The Life and Fate of the Ancient Library of Alexandria*. Paris, France: UNESCO, 1990.
Ellis, William. *Polynesian Researches*. London, UK: Fisher, Son, and Jackson, 1831.
Epiphanius. *Panarion*. Frank Williams, trans. Leiden, Netherlands: Brill, 1987.
Estete, Miguel de. *Relation of the Discovery of the Kingdom of Peru*. In *Narratives of the Conquest of Peru*. Clements R. Markham, ed. London, UK: Hakluyt Society, 1873.
Euripides. *Iphigenia in Aulis*. London, UK: Penguin Classics, 2003.
Eusebius. *The Ecclesiastical History*. London, UK: George Bell and Sons, 1885.
Evans, Sebastian. *The High History of the Holy Graal*. London, UK: J. M. Dent and Company, 1898.
Evans, J. Gwenogvryn, ed. *Brut y Tywysogion: Or The Chronicle of the Princes*. London, UK: Humphrey Milford, 1910.
Evans, Arthur. *The Palace of Minos*. London, UK: Macmillan, 1909.
Faber, Harold. *The Mystery of the Amber Room*. New York: Random House, 1975.
Farrar, Frederic W. *The Early Days of Christianity*. London, UK: Cassell, 1882.
Fisher, John H. *Confederate Treasury Records: A Guide to the Official Archives*. Richmond, VA: Virginia State Library, 1964.
Foerstemann, Ernst Wilhelm. *Commentary on the Maya Manuscript in the Royal Public Library of Dresden*. Dresden, Germany: Royal Public Library, 1880.
Foley, Arthur. *Arthur Conan Doyle: A Critical Study*. London, UK: Chapman and Hall, 1912.
Françoise, Henry and G. L. Marsh-Micheli. *The Book of Kells: Reproductions from the Manuscript in Trinity College Dublin with a Study of the Manuscript by Françoise Henry*. New York: Alfred A. Knopf, 1974.

Freeth, Tony. *The Antikythera Mechanism: Decoding an Ancient Greek Astronomical Calculator*. Cambridge, MA: Harvard University Press, 2019.
Gad, Finn. *The History of Greenland, Volume I: Earliest Times to 1700*. London, UK: C. Hurst & Company, 1970.
Gamble, Harry Y. *The New Testament Canon: Its Making and Meaning*. Philadelphia, PA: Fortress Press, 1985.
Gardiner, Alan H. *Egyptian Grammar*. Oxford, UK: Oxford University Press, 1927.
Gardiner, Henry. *The Ancient History of the Near East from the Earliest Times to the Battle of Salamis*. London, UK: Edward Arnold, 1901.
Gaster, Theodore H. *The Dead Sea Scriptures*. New York: Doubleday, 1956.
Gates, William. *An Outline Dictionary of Maya Glyphs*. Baltimore, MD: The Maya Society, 1931.
Geminus. *Elements of Astronomy*. London, UK: John W. Parker, 1852.
Gibbon, Edward. *The History of the Decline and Fall of the Roman Empire*. London, UK: Strahan and Cadell, 1776.
Gill, Christopher. *Plato's Atlantis Story: Text, Translation, and Commentary*. Liverpool, UK: Liverpool University Press, 2017.
Gilmour-Bryson, Anne. *The Trial of the Templars in Cyprus*. Leiden, Netherlands: Brill, 1998.
Gísli Sigurðsson. *The Medieval Icelandic Saga and Oral Tradition: A Discourse on Method*. Cambridge, MA: Harvard University Press, 2004.
Gjerløw, Ludvig. *Liturgica Norvegica*. Oslo, Norway: Universitetsforlaget, 1964.
Gladwin, Thomas. *East Is a Big Bird: Navigation and Logic on Puluwat Atoll*. Cambridge, MA: Harvard University Press, 1970.
Goodspeed, Edgar J. *A History of Early Christian Literature*. Chicago, IL: University of Chicago Press, 1942.
Goodwin, William W. *The Greek Fathers of the Church*. Boston, MA: Ginn and Company, 1900.
Gosden, Chris and Chantal Conneller, eds. *The Oxford Handbook of the Archaeology of the Arctic*. Oxford, UK: Oxford University Press, 2022.
Grant, Michael. *Myths of the Greeks and Romans*. New York: Penguin Classics, 1962.
Graziosi, Barbara, and Johannes Haubold, eds. *Homer: Iliad Book VI*. Cambridge, UK: Cambridge University Press, 2010.
Green, Miranda. *The Archaeology of Celtic Art*. London, UK: Routledge, 1996.
—. *Boudica and Her Story*. London, UK: Thames and Hudson, 1997.
Griffin Murray, Rachel. *The Book of Kells: Explorations of an Irish Masterpiece*. Cork, Ireland: Cork University Press, 2012.
Grote, George. *A History of Greece*. London, UK: John Murray, 1846.
Grousset, René. *Histoire des Croisades et du Royaume Franc de Jérusalem*. Paris, France: Plon, 1934.
Grove, Jonathan. "The Norse in Greenland." In *The Oxford Illustrated History of the Vikings*, Peter Sawyer, ed. Oxford, UK: Oxford University Press, 1997.
Guðbrandur Vigfússon, and F. York Powell, eds. *Origines Islandicae: A Collection of the More Important Sagas and Other Native Writings Relating to the Settlement and Early History of Iceland*. Oxford, UK: Clarendon Press, 1905.
Guerber, H. A. *The Myths of Greece and Rome*. London, UK: George G. Harrap, 1893.
Guillaume de Nangis. *Chronique Latine de Guillaume de Nangis*. Paris: Imprimerie Nationale, 1843.
Gulson, George. *The Hebrew Text of the Old Testament*. London, UK: Society for Promoting Christian Knowledge, 1878.
Gurney, Oliver. *The Hittites*. Harmondsworth, UK: Penguin, 1952.
Guthrie, Kenneth S. *The Message of the Masters*. New York: Brentano's, 1926.
Gwynn, Edward J. *The Book of Kells*. Dublin, Ireland: Royal Irish Academy, 1914.
Halldórsson, Ólafur. *Grænlandsferðir biskupa*. Reykjavík, Iceland: Hið íslenzka bókmenntafélag, 1978.
Halliday, F. E. *A Shakespeare Companion 1564–1964*. New York: Viking Press, 1964.

Harnack, Adolf von. *The History of Dogma*. London, England: Williams and Norgate, 1894.
—. *History of Early Christian Literature to the End of the Second Century*. London, UK: Williams and Norgate, 1894.
—. *The Expansion of Christianity in the First Three Centuries*. James Moffatt, trans. New York: G.P. Putnam's Sons, 1904.
—. *The Mission and Expansion of Christianity*. London, England: Williams and Norgate, 1908.
—. *The Sayings of Jesus*. London, England: Williams and Norgate, 1908.
Hartwig, Otto. *Die Kunstschätze der Zaren*. Leipzig, Germany: Brockhaus, 1899.
Hatch, Edwin. *The Organisation of the Early Christian Churches*. London, UK: Rivingtons, 1881.
Hatto, A. T., trans. *Das Nibelungenlied*. London, UK: Penguin Classics, 1965.
Haverfield, F. *The Romanization of Roman Britain*. London, UK: Clarendon Press, 1905.
Hawley, W. M. *Japanese Swordsmiths*. Hollywood, CA: W. M. Hawley, 1966.
Haynes, Sybille. *Etruscan Civilization: A Cultural History*. Los Angeles, CA: Getty Publications, 2000.
Hegesippus. Fragments. In *The Apostolic Fathers*. Michael W. Holmes, ed. Grand Rapids, MI: Baker Academic, 2007.
Helm, Robert. *Lost Gold of the Dutchman Mine*. Phoenix, AZ: Southwest Press, 1936.
Hemming, John. *The Conquest of the Incas*. New York: Harcourt Brace Jovanovich, 1970.
Henry, Peter. *Sappho and Her Latest Discoveries*. London, UK: Faber and Faber, 1928.
Herbert, Joan. *The Quest for the Holy Grail: Studies in Medieval Tradition*. London, UK: Methuen and Company, 1931.
Higham, Charles. *The Adventures of Conan Doyle: The Life of the Creator of Sherlock Holmes*. New York: W. W. Norton and Company, 1976.
Hingley, Richard. *Boudica: Iron Age Warrior Queen*. London, UK: Bloomsbury Academic, 2006.
Hingley, Richard, and Christina Unwin. *Boudica: The British Revolt Against Rome AD 60*. Oxford, UK: Oxbow Books, 2005.
Hodgson, Nick. "The End of the Ninth Legion, War in Britain, and the Building of Hadrian's Wall." *Britannia* 52. London, UK: Society for the Promotion of Roman Studies, 2021.
Holmes, T. S. *The Origin and Development of the Eucharistic Chalice*. London, UK: Society for Promoting Christian Knowledge, 1912.
Homer. *The Iliad*. London, UK: Penguin Classics, 1990.
Hornung, Erik. *Conceptions of God in Ancient Egypt*. John Baines, trans. Ithaca, NY: Cornell University Press, 1982.
Hort, Fenton John Anthony. *Two Dissertations*. London, UK: Macmillan and Co., 1876.
Hough, Richard. *Captain James Cook: A Biography*. New York: W. W. Norton, 1995.
How and Wells, eds. *A Commentary on Herodotus*. Oxford, UK: Clarendon Press, 1912.
Howarth, Stephen. *The Knights Templar*. New York: Atheneum, 1982.
Howorth, Henry H. *History of the Mongols: From the 9th to the 19th Century; Part II: The Mongols of Persia*. London, UK: Longmans, Green, and Co., 1880.
Hrdlička, Aleš. *Early Man in Siberia*. Washington, D.C.: Smithsonian Institution, 1920.
Hyde, James Wilson. *The Templars in Scotland*. Edinburgh, Scotland: David Douglas, 1903.
Jackson, Peter. *The Viking Age: A Reader*. Toronto, Canada: University of Toronto Press, 2013.
Jacobsen, Thorkild. *The Sumerian King List*. Chicago, IL: University of Chicago Press, 1939.
Jebb, Richard Claverhouse. *The Attic Orators from Antiphon to Isaeus*. London, UK: Macmillan, 1893.
Jenkins, J. Geraint. *The Celts and the Welsh: The Making of a Nation*. Stroud, UK: Tempus Publishing, 2005.
Jerome. *Commentary on Matthew*. Oxford, UK: Parker, 1848.

Jerome. *Lives of Illustrious Men*. Ernest Cushing Richardson, trans. New York: Christian Literature Company, 1892.
Jones, Thomas. *Brut y Tywysogyon: Peniarth MS 20 Version*. Cardiff, Wales: University of Wales Press, 1952.
Josephus, Flavius. *The Antiquities of the Jews*. New York: Harper and Brothers, 1851.
—. *The Jewish War*. Cambridge, MA: Harvard University Press, 1927.
Joy, J. *Celtic Gilded Metalwork*. London, UK: British Museum Press, 2010.
Joyce, Patrick Weston. *The Origin and History of Irish Names of Places*. Dublin, Ireland: McGlashan and Gill, 1869.
Juvaini, Ata-Malik. *The History of the World-Conqueror*. J. A. Boyle, trans. Manchester, UK: Manchester University Press, 1958.
Kanzan, Sato. *The Japanese Sword: A Detailed Study of the Blade*. Tokyo: Kodansha International, 1983.
Kendrick, T. D. *The Druids: A Study in Celtic Prehistory*. London, UK: Methuen, 1927.
Kenyon, Frederic G. *Handbook to the Textual Criticism of the New Testament*. London, UK: Macmillan and Co., 1901.
Kenyon, Frederic G. *Our Bible and the Ancient Manuscripts*. London, UK: Eyre and Spottiswoode, 1895.
Kenyon, Frederic G. *Our Bible and the Ancient Manuscripts*. London, UK: Eyre & Spottiswoode, 1895.
Keppie, Lawrence. *Understanding Roman Inscriptions*. Baltimore, MD: Johns Hopkins University Press, 1991.
—. *The Making of the Roman Army: From Republic to Empire*. Norman, OK: University of Oklahoma Press, 1998.
Kern, Hendrik. *Manual of Indian Buddhism*. Delhi, India: Motilal Banarsidass, 1981.
Khenzykhenova, F. V. *Ancient Cultures of the Altai Mountains*. Leningrad, Russia: Nauka, 1977.
Kiernan, Kevin S. *Beowulf and the Beowulf Manuscript*. New Brunswick, NJ: Rutgers University Press, 1981.
King, James. *A Voyage to the Pacific Ocean*. London, UK: G. Nicol and T. Cadell, 1784.
Klaeber, Friedrich, ed. *Beowulf and the Fight at Finnsburg*. Boston, MA: D.C. Heath and Company, 1950.
Klauck, Hans-Josef. *Apocryphal Gospels: An Introduction*. Waco, TX: Baylor University Press, 2003.
Klijn, Albertus F. J. *Jewish-Christian Gospel Tradition*. Leiden, Netherlands: Brill, 1992.
Knowles, David. *Christian Worship and the Early Church*. London, UK: Longmans, Green and Company, 1947.
Koenen, Ludwig. *Griechische Papyri aus Ägypten*. Leipzig, Germany: Teubner, 1892.
Koester, Helmut. *Ancient Christian Gospels: Their History and Development*. Philadelphia, PA: Trinity Press International, 1990.
Kollenborn, Tom. *Superstition Mountain: A Ride Through Time*. Apache Junction, AZ: Superstition Mountain Historical Society, 2012.
Kramer, Samuel Noah. *The Sumerians: Their History, Culture, and Character*. Chicago, IL: University of Chicago Press, 1963.
Krause, Johannes. *A Short History of Humanity: A New History of Old Europe*. New York: Random House, 2021.
Krause, Johannes, and Thomas Higham. *Ancient Bones: Unearthing the Dawn of Modern Humans*. New York: Random House, 2021.
Krogh, Knud J. *Gardar: The Episcopal See of the Norsemen in Greenland*. Copenhagen, Denmark: The National Museum of Denmark, 1982.
Kühn, Erich. *Bernstein: Ein Weltstoff der Ostsee*. Berlin, Germany: Dietrich Reimer, 1924.
Kyle, Melvin Grove, and Albright, William Foxwell. *Archaeology and the Bible*. Philadelphia, PA: The Sunday School Times Company, 1915.
Lactantius. *Divinae Institutiones*. Mary Francis McDonald, trans. Washington, D.C.: Catholic University of America Press, 1964.
Lake, Kirsopp. *Codex Sinaiticus Petropolitanus: The New Testament, the Epistle of Barnabas,*

and the Shepherd of Hermas. Oxford, UK: Clarendon Press, 1911.
Landa, Diego de. Relación de las Cosas de Yucatán. 1566. Madrid, Spain: Ediciones Aguilar, 1959.
Lane, George. Genghis Khan and Mongol Rule. Santa Barbara, CA: Greenwood Press, 2009.
Langdon, Stephen. Historical and Religious Texts from the Cuneiform Sources. Paris: Geuthner, 1912.
Layard, Austen Henry. Nineveh and Its Remains. London, England: John Murray, 1849.
Layton, Bentley, ed. The Gnostic Scriptures: A New Translation with Annotations and Introductions. New York, NY: Doubleday, 1987.
Lee, Sidney. A Life of William Shakespeare. London, UK: Smith, Elder and Company, 1898.
León-Portilla, Miguel (ed.). The Broken Spears: The Aztec Account of the Conquest of Mexico. Boston, MA: Beacon Press, 1962.
Lewis, David. We, the Navigators: The Ancient Art of Landfinding in the Pacific. Honolulu, HI: University of Hawaii Press, 1972.
Li, Rongxi (trans.). The Great Tang Records on the Western Regions. Berkeley, CA: Numata Center for Buddhist Translation, 1996.
Lightfoot, J. B. Essays on Supernatural Religion. London, UK: Macmillan, 1889.
—. The Apostolic Fathers: Clement, Ignatius, and Polycarp. London, UK: Macmillan, 1891.
Lindow, John. Norse Mythology: A Guide to the Gods, Heroes, Rituals, and Beliefs. Oxford, UK: Oxford University Press, 2001.
Lisiansky, Urey. A Voyage Round the World in the Years 1803, 1804, 1805, and 1806. London, UK: John Booth, 1814.
Livy. History of Rome. Cambridge, MA: Harvard University Press, 1919.
Livy. Ab Urbe Condita. Benjamin Oliver Foster, trans. Cambridge, MA: Harvard University Press, 1919.
Lloyd, Alan B. Herodotus Book II: Commentary. Leiden, Netherlands: Brill, 1976.
Lloyd, John Edward. A History of Wales from the Earliest Times to the Edwardian Conquest. London, UK: Longmans, Green, and Company, 1911.
Lobel, Edgar, and Denys Page, eds. Poetarum Lesbiorum Fragmenta. Oxford, UK: Clarendon Press, 1955.
Lührmann, Dieter. Die apokryph gewordenen Evangelien: Studien zu neuen Texten und zu neuen Fragen. Tübingen, Germany: Mohr Siebeck, 2000.
Lynch, Ann K. Medieval Welsh Society: Selected Studies. Cardiff, Wales: University of Wales Press, 1978.
Magini, Massimo. The Pyrgi Tablets: Etruscan and Phoenician Texts in Gold. Florence, Italy: Olschki, 2005.
Magnússon, Sigurður, and Axel Bolvig, eds. Den grønlandske kirkes historie i middelalderen. Copenhagen, Denmark: Gyldendal, 1984.
Mahaffy, J. P. The Empire of the Ptolemies. London, UK: Macmillan, 1895.
Marchant, Jo. Decoding the Heavens: A 2,000-Year-Old Computer and the Century-Long Search to Discover Its Secrets. New York: Da Capo Press, 2008.
Marlowe, Christopher. The Complete Works of Christopher Marlowe. London, UK: J. M. Dent and Company, 1900.
Mason, R. H. Art Treasures of Europe. London, England: Methuen and Company, 1931.
Maspero, Gaston. History of Egypt, Chaldea, Syria, Babylonia, and Assyria. London, UK: Grolier Society, 1903.
Max Müller, F. Sacred Books of the East. Oxford, UK: Clarendon Press, 1879.
Meehan, Bernard. The Book of Kells: An Illustrated Introduction to the Manuscript in Trinity College Dublin. London, UK: Thames and Hudson, 2012.
Metzger, Bruce M. The Early Versions of the New Testament: Their Origin, Transmission, and Limitations. Oxford, UK: Oxford University Press, 1977.
—. The Canon of the New Testament: Its Origin, Development, and Significance. Oxford, UK: Oxford University Press, 1987.
Metzger, Bruce M., and Bart D. Ehrman. The Text of the New Testament: Its Transmission,

Corruption, and Restoration. Oxford, UK: Oxford University Press, 2005.
Meyer, Marvin, ed. *The Nag Hammadi Scriptures*. New York: HarperOne, 2009.
Michaud, Joseph François. *Histoire des Croisades*. Paris: Firmin Didot, 1841.
Michelet, Jules. *Procès des Templiers*. Paris: Imprimerie Nationale, 1841.
Millar, Fergus. *The Roman Near East, 31 BC–AD 337*. Cambridge, UK: Harvard University Press, 1993.
Milligan, George. *The New Testament Documents: Their Origin and Early History*. London, UK: Macmillan and Co., 1913.
Milne, H. J. M., and T. C. Skeat. *Scribes and Correctors of the Codex Sinaiticus*. London, UK: British Museum, 1938.
Mitra, Rajendralal. *The Sanskrit Buddhist Literature of Nepal*. Calcutta, India: Asiatic Society of Bengal, 1882.
Moloney, Alfred. *Sketches of the Island of Cocos in the Pacific Ocean*. London, UK: G. Street, 1875.
Mommsen, Theodor. *The History of Rome*. New York: Scribner, 1868.
Mor, M. "Two Legions – The Same Fate? The Disappearance of the Legions IX Hispana and XXII Deiotariana." *Zeitschrift für Papyrologie und Epigraphik* 62. Bonn, Germany: Habelt, 1986.
Moraldi, Luigi, ed. *The Complete Gospels of Jesus Christ*. New York: Doubleday, 1986.
Morgan, David. *The Mongols*. Oxford, UK: Blackwell, 1986.
Morley, Sylvanus Griswold. *An Introduction to the Study of the Maya Hieroglyphs*. Washington, D.C.: Bureau of American Ethnology, 1915.
Morrell, Benjamin. *A Narrative of Four Voyages: Being a Series of Adventures in the South Sea, North and South Pacific Ocean, Chinese Sea, Ethiopic and Southern Atlantic Ocean, Indian and Antarctic Ocean*. New York: J. and J. Harper, 1832.
Morris, William, trans. *The Story of the Volsungs and Niblungs*. London, UK: Reeves and Turner, 1870.
Moss, H. St. L. B. *The Birth of the Middle Ages, 395–814*. Oxford, UK: Clarendon Press, 1935.
Nagayama, Kōkan. *The Connoisseur's Book of Japanese Swords*. Tokyo: Kodansha International, 1997.
Napier, Arthur Sampson, ed. *Old English Glosses: Chiefly Unpublished*. Oxford, UK: Clarendon Press, 1900.
Nestle, Eberhard. *Introduction to the Textual Criticism of the New Testament*. London, UK: Williams and Norgate, 1901.
Nicholson, Helen J. *The Knights Templar: A New History*. Stroud, UK: Sutton Publishing, 2001.
Nørlund, Poul. *Brattahlid: The Home of Eric the Red*. Copenhagen, Denmark: Levin and Munksgaard, 1934.
Norton, Christopher. *St William of York*. York, UK: York Medieval Press, 2006.
O'Neill, Henry. *Illustrations of the Most Interesting of the Sculptured Crosses of Ancient Ireland*. London, UK: Chapman and Hall, 1859.
O'Reilly, Bernard. *Cocos Island: Its History, Nature and Treasures*. London, UK: T. Fisher Unwin, 1891.
Okazaki, Katsusaburō. *Studies in Old Japanese Swords*. Tokyo: Maruzen, 1912.
Ólason, Vésteinn. *Dialogues with the Viking Age: Narration and Representation in the Sagas of Icelanders*. Reykjavík, Iceland: Heimskringla, 1998.
Origen. *Commentary on Matthew*. Cambridge, UK: Cambridge University Press, 1896.
Orosius, Paulus. *Seven Books of History Against the Pagans*. Roy J. Deferrari, trans. Washington, D.C.: Catholic University of America Press, 1964.
Owen, Aneurin, ed. *Ancient Laws and Institutes of Wales*. London, UK: Record Commission, 1841.
Pääbo, Svante. *Neanderthal Man: In Search of Lost Genomes*. New York: Basic Books, 2014.
Pääbo, Svante. *A Neanderthal Perspective on Human Origins*. Berkeley, CA: University of California Press, 2013.
Pagels, Elaine. *The Gnostic Gospels*. New York, NY: Vintage, 1981.

Pallottino, Massimo. *The Etruscans.* Bloomington, IN: Indiana University Press, 1975.
Paris, Matthew. *Chronica Majora.* London, UK: Longman & Co., 1877.
Parker, H. M. D. *The Roman Legions.* Oxford, UK: Clarendon Press, 1928.
Pearson, Hesketh. *Conan Doyle: His Life and Art.* London, UK: Methuen and Company, 1931.
Perkins, Pheme. *Gnosticism and the New Testament.* Minneapolis, MN: Fortress Press, 1993.
Petrie, Flinders. *Tombs of the Courtiers and Oxyrhynchus Papyri.* London, UK: Egypt Exploration Fund, 1897.
Pfeiffer, Robert H. *History of New Testament Times.* New York: Harper and Brothers, 1949.
Pfiffig, Ambros Josef. *Religione degli Etruschi.* Florence, Italy: Sansoni, 1975.
Philo of Byzantium. *The Seven Wonders of the World.* Jean Blackwood, trans. Edinburgh, Scotland: Edinburgh University Press, 1898.
Pizarro, Pedro. "Relation of the Discovery and Conquest of the Kingdoms of Peru." In *Narratives of the Conquest of Peru.* Clements R. Markham, ed. London, UK: Hakluyt Society, 1873.
Plato. *Timaeus and Critias.* Robin Waterfield, trans. Oxford, UK: Oxford University Press, 2008.
Pliny the Elder. *The Natural History.* London, UK: Henry G. Bohn, 1855.
Plutarch. *Plutarch's Lives.* Bernadotte Perrin, trans. London, UK: William Heinemann, 1914.
—. *Moralia.* Frank Cole Babbitt, trans. London, UK: William Heinemann, 1927.
Pollard, Alfred. *Shakespeare Folios and Quartos: A Study in the Bibliography of Shakespeare's Plays.* London, UK: Methuen and Company, 1909.
Polybius. *The Histories.* London, UK: Macmillan, 1889.
Poole, Reginald Stuart. *The Cities of Egypt.* London, UK: Society for Promoting Christian Knowledge, 1882.
Poseidippos of Pella. *Epigrams.* A. S. F. Gow and D. L. Page, trans. Cambridge, UK: Cambridge University Press, 1965.
Pressouyre, Léon. *Le Rêve de Pierre: Essai sur l'Architecture Templier.* Paris: Éditions du CNRS, 1999.
Price, Derek de Solla. *Gears from the Greeks: The Antikythera Mechanism—A Calendar Computer from ca. 80 B.C.* New York: Science History Publications, 1974.
Puech, Émile. *Fragments évangéliques judéo-chrétiens.* Paris: Cerf, 1987.
Quispel, Gilles. *Gnosis als Weltreligion.* Zürich, Switzerland: Origo, 1951.
—. ed. *The Gospel of Thomas and the Gospel of the Egyptians.* Leiden, Netherlands: Brill, 1957.
Ralls, Karen. *The Templars and the Grail: Knights of the Quest.* Wheaton, IL: Quest Books, 2003.
Rashid al-Din. *Jāmiʿ al-Tawārīkh: Compendium of Chronicles.* Wheeler M. Thackston, trans. Cambridge, MA: Harvard University, Department of Near Eastern Languages and Civilizations, 1998.
Ratchnevsky, Paul. *Genghis Khan: His Life and Legacy.* Thomas Nivison Haining, trans. Oxford, UK: Blackwell, 1991.
Rauch, Georg. *Kunstschätze des Alten Preußen.* Leipzig, Germany: Koehler and Amelang, 1927.
Raymond, Wayland D. *The Germanic Heroic Legend: A Critical Study.* New York: Houghton Mifflin, 1912.
Read, Piers Paul. *The Templars.* New York: St. Martin's Press, 1999.
Rehm, Albert. *Ancient Greek Astronomy and the Mechanical Tradition.* Munich, Germany: Akademische Verlagsgesellschaft, 1902.
Reich, David. *Who We Are and How We Got Here: Ancient DNA and the New Science of the Human Past.* New York: Pantheon Books, 2018.
Reinach, Théodore. *A History of Antiquity: The Orient and Greece.* London, UK: William Heinemann, 1907.

Renan, Ernest. *The Life of Jesus.* London, UK: Trübner and Company, 1864.
Rendall, Gerald H. *Solon the Athenian.* London, UK: George Bell and Sons, 1927.
Rhys, John. *Celtic Britain.* London, UK: Society for Promoting Christian Knowledge, 1882.
Rickman, John. *Journal of Captain Cook's Last Voyage to the Pacific Ocean.* London, UK: Messrs. T. and J. Egerton, 1781.
Riley-Smith, Jonathan. *The Crusades: A Short History.* New Haven, CT: Yale University Press, 1987.
Ritter-Schaumburg, Walter. *Die Nibelungen sind Schwaben: Untersuchungen über Herkunft und Schauplätze der Nibelungensage.* Stuttgart, Germany: Konrad Theiss Verlag, 1973.
Ritterling, Emil. "Legio IX Hispana." In *Realencyclopädie der Classischen Altertumswissenschaft,* Georg Wissowa, ed. Stuttgart, Germany: J. B. Metzler, 1925.
Rix, Helmut, ed. *Etruskische Texte.* Tübingen, Germany: Gunter Narr Verlag, 1991.
Robertson, A. T. *An Introduction to the Textual Criticism of the New Testament.* London, UK: Hodder and Stoughton, 1925.
Robinson, Edward. *Biblical Researches in Palestine, Mount Sinai and Arabia Petraea.* London, UK: John Murray, 1841.
Robinson, James M., ed. *The Nag Hammadi Library in English.* San Francisco, CA: Harper & Row, 1977.
Roesdahl, Else. *The Vikings.* London, UK: Penguin Books, 1998.
Rogers, Richard A. *Stone Age Siberia: Human Origins in the Glacial North.* London, UK: Thames and Hudson, 1969.
Roller, Duane W. *Ancient Geography: The Discovery of the World in Classical Greece and Rome.* London, UK: I. B. Tauris, 2015.
Through the Pillars of Herakles: Greco-Roman Exploration of the Atlantic. London, UK: Routledge, 2006.
Romer, John. *A History of Ancient Egypt, Volume 2: From the Great Pyramid to the Fall of the Middle Kingdom.* New York: St. Martin's Press, 2017.
Rose, H. J. *A Handbook of Greek Mythology.* London, UK: Methuen, 1928.
Ross, Anne. *Pagan Celtic Britain: Studies in Iconography and Tradition.* London, UK: Routledge, 1967.
Roux, Jean-Paul. *Genghis Khan and the Mongol Empire.* New York: Harry N. Abrams, 2003.
Rowley, H. H. *The Zadokite Fragments and the Dead Sea Scrolls.* Oxford, UK: Basil Blackwell, 1952.
Runciman, Steven. *A History of the Crusades.* Cambridge, UK: Cambridge University Press, 1951.
Russo, Alessandra. *Le Lamine Auree dell'Italia Antica: Testi, Cultura, e Religione.* Rome, Italy: Quasar, 2012.
Saggs, H. W. F. *The Greatness That Was Babylon.* New York: Hawthorn Books, 1962.
Sahagún, Bernardino de. *Florentine Codex: General History of the Things of New Spain.* Santa Fe, NM: School of American Research, 1950.
Santi, Maria Paola. *Scrittura e Potere nell'Etruria Antica.* Pisa, Italy: Edizioni ETS, 2018.
Sarton, George. *Ancient Science Through the Golden Age of Greece.* New York: Dover Publications, 1959.
Satō, Kazan. *Kamakura Swordsmiths and Their Schools.* Tokyo: Yūzankaku, 1926.
Sayce, Archibald Henry. *The Ancient Empires of the East.* London, UK: Religious Tract Society, 1884.
—. *Lectures on the Origin and Growth of Religion as Illustrated by the Religion of the Ancient Babylonians.* London, UK: Williams and Norgate, 1887.
Sayce, R. U. *Primitive Ritual and Burial Customs of Northern Eurasia.* London, UK: Macmillan, 1908.
Schechter, Solomon. *Documents of Jewish Sectaries.* Cambridge, UK: Cambridge University Press, 1910.
Schleiermacher, Friedrich. *Critical Essay on the Gospel of Luke.* London, England: Williams

and Norgate, 1825.
—. *On Religion: Speeches to Its Cultured Despisers*. London, England: Kegan Paul, 1893.
—. *The Christian Faith: A Systematic Presentation*. Edinburgh, Scotland: T. and T. Clark, 1893.
—. *The Christian Faith*. New York: Harper and Brothers, 1928.
Schliemann, Heinrich. *Mycenae: A Narrative of Researches and Discoveries*. London, UK: John Murray, 1878.
Schneemelcher, Wilhelm, ed. *New Testament Apocrypha, Volume 1: Gospels and Related Writings*. Louisville, KY: Westminster John Knox Press, 1991.
Schoeps, Hans-Joachim. *Jewish Christianity: Factional Disputes in the Early Church*. London, UK: Lutterworth Press, 1969.
Schopen, Gregory. *Buddhist Monks and Business Matters: Still More Papers on Monastic Buddhism in India*. Honolulu, HI: University of Hawai'i Press, 2004.
Schottmüller, Konrad. *Der Untergang des Templerordens*. Munich, Germany: J. F. Lehmanns Verlag, 1930.
Scrivener, F. H. A. *A Plain Introduction to the Criticism of the New Testament*. London, UK: George Bell and Sons, 1883.
Seabrook, Lochlainn. *Aphrodite's Trade: The Hidden History of Prostitution Unveiled*. 1994. Franklin, TN: Sea Raven Press, 2011 ed.
—. *The Goddess Dictionary of Words and Phrases: Introducing a New Core Vocabulary for the Women's Spirituality Movement*. 1997. Franklin, TN: Sea Raven Press, 2010 ed.
—. *Britannia Rules: Goddess-Worship in Ancient Anglo-Celtic Society - An Academic Look at the United Kingdom's Matricentric Spiritual Past*. 1999. Franklin, TN: Sea Raven Press, 2010 ed.
—. *The Book of Kelle: An Introduction to Goddess-Worship and the Great Celtic Mother-Goddess Kelle, Original Blessed Lady of Ireland*. 1999. Franklin, TN: Sea Raven Press, 2010 ed.
—. *Christmas Before Christianity: How the Birthday of the "Sun" Became the Birthday of the "Son."* Franklin, TN: Sea Raven Press, 2010.
—. *Everything You Were Taught About the Civil War is Wrong, Ask a Southerner!* 2010. Franklin, TN: Sea Raven Press, 2024 ed.
—. *The Quotable Jefferson Davis: Selections From the Writings and Speeches of the Confederacy's First President*. Franklin, TN: Sea Raven Press, 2011.
—. *Honest Jeff and Dishonest Abe: A Southern Children's Guide to the Civil War*. Franklin, TN: Sea Raven Press, 2012.
—. *Christ Is All and In All: Rediscovering Your Divine Nature and the Kingdom Within*. Franklin, TN: Sea Raven Press, 2014.
—. *Jesus and the Gospel of Q: Christ's Pre-Christian Teachings as Recorded in the New Testament*. Franklin, TN: Sea Raven Press, 2014.
—. *Confederate Blood and Treasure: An Interview With Lochlainn Seabrook*. Spring Hill, TN: Sea Raven Press, 2015.
—. *Confederacy 101: Amazing Facts You Never Knew About America's Oldest Political Tradition*. Spring Hill, TN: Sea Raven Press, 2015.
—. *Slavery 101: Amazing Facts You Never Knew About America's "Peculiar Institution."* Spring Hill, TN: Sea Raven Press, 2015.
—. *Confederate Flag Facts: What Every American Should Know About Dixie's Southern Cross*. Spring Hill, TN: Sea Raven Press, 2016.
—. *Seabrook's Bible Dictionary of Traditional and Mystical Christian Doctrines*. Spring Hill, TN: Sea Raven Press, 2016.
—. *Lincoln's War: The Real Cause, the Real Winner, the Real Loser*. Spring Hill, TN: Sea Raven Press, 2016.
—. *Abraham Lincoln Was a Liberal, Jefferson Davis Was a Conservative: The Missing Key to Understanding the American Civil War*. Spring Hill, TN: Sea Raven Press, 2017.
—. *All We Ask is to be Let Alone: The Southern Secession Fact Book*. Spring Hill, TN: Sea Raven Press, 2017.
—. *The Ultimate Civil War Quiz Book: How Much Do You Really Know About America's Most*

Misunderstood Conflict? Spring Hill, TN: Sea Raven Press, 2017.
——. *Confederate Monuments: Why Every American Should Honor Confederate Soldiers and Their Memorials.* Spring Hill, TN: Sea Raven Press, 2018.
——. (ed.) *A Short History of the Confederate States of America* (Jefferson Davis, Belford Company, NY, 1890). A Sea Raven Press Reprint. Spring Hill, TN: Sea Raven Press, 2020.
——. (ed.) *Prison Life of Jefferson Davis: Embracing Details and Incidents in his Captivity, With Conversations on Topics of Public Interest* (John J. Craven, Sampson, Low, Son, and Marston, London, UK, 1866). A Sea Raven Press Reprint. Spring Hill, TN: Sea Raven Press, 2020.
——. *Heroes of the Southern Confederacy: The Illustrated Book of Confederate Officials, Soldiers, and Civilians.* Spring Hill, TN: Sea Raven Press, 2021.
——. (ed.) *The Rise and Fall of the Confederate Government* (Jefferson Davis, D. Appleton, New York, 1881). 2 vols. A Sea Raven Press Facsimile Reprint. Spring Hill, TN: Sea Raven Press, 2022.
——. *Secrets of Celebrity Surnames: An Onomastic Dictionary of Famous People.* Cody, WY: Sea Raven Press, 2023.
——. *I, Confederate: Why Dixie Seceded and Fought in the Words of Southern Soldiers.* Spring Hill, TN: Sea Raven Press, 2023.
——. *The Greatest Jesus Mystery of All Time: Where Was Christ Between the Ages of 12 and 30?* Cody, WY: Sea Raven Press, 2024.
——. *Manmade: Male Inventors Who Created the Modern World.* Cody, WY: Sea Raven Press, 2025.
——. *Jesus and the Gospel of Thomas: A Christian Mystic's View of Christianity's Most Important Ancient Text.* Cody, WY: Sea Raven Press, 2025.
Seaver, Kirsten A. *The Frozen Echo: Greenland and the Exploration of North America, ca. A.D. 1000–1500.* Stanford, CA: Stanford University Press, 1996.
Sesko, Markus. *Encyclopedia of Japanese Swords.* Portland, OR: Lulu Press, 2014.
Setton, Kenneth M., ed. *A History of the Crusades.* Madison, WI: University of Wisconsin Press, 1955.
Sheppard, Si. *Roman Britain: A History from Julius Caesar to the Departure of the Romans.* Oxford, UK: Osprey Publishing, 2016.
Shirer, William L. *The Rise and Fall of the Third Reich: A History of Nazi Germany.* New York: Simon and Schuster, 1960.
Shunkov, Mikhail V. *Denisova Cave: Archaeology and Paleogenetics.* Novosibirsk, Russia: Siberian Branch of the Russian Academy of Sciences Press, 2015.
Sijpesteijn, P. J. "Die Legio Nona Hispana in Nimwegen." *Zeitschrift für Papyrologie und Epigraphik* 111. Bonn, Germany: Habelt, 1996.
Simek, Rudolf. *Dictionary of Northern Mythology.* Cambridge, UK: D. S. Brewer, 1993.
Simpson, Elizabeth, ed. *The Spoils of War: The Loss, Reappearance, and Recovery of Cultural Property.* New York: Harry N. Abrams, 1997.
Singer, Charles Joseph. *A Short History of Scientific Ideas to 1900.* London, UK: Oxford University Press, 1928.
Smith, George Adam. *The Historical Geography of the Holy Land.* London, England: Hodder and Stoughton, 1894.
Smith, Irwin. *Shakespeare's Blackfriars Playhouse: Its History and Its Design.* New York: New York University Press, 1964.
Smith, Michael E. *The Aztecs.* Oxford, UK: Blackwell Publishers, 1996.
Smith, Morton. *The Secret Gospel: The Discovery and Interpretation of the Secret Gospel According to Mark.* New York: Harper & Row, 1973.
——. *Clement of Alexandria and a Secret Gospel of Mark.* Cambridge, UK: Harvard University Press, 1973.
Smith, Timothy H. *The Real Treasure of the Confederacy.* Macon, GA: Mercer University Press, 1994.
Smith, William, ed. *Dictionary of Greek and Roman Biography and Mythology.* London, UK: John Murray, 1873.

Snell, Bruno. *Die Entdeckung des Geistes: Studien zur Entstehung des europäischen Denkens bei den Griechen*. Hamburg, Germany: Claassen Verlag, 1946.
Spalinger, Anthony. *War in Ancient Egypt: The New Kingdom*. Oxford, UK: Blackwell, 2005.
Spuler, Bertold. *The Mongol Empire: Its Rise and Legacy*. London, UK: Bruno Cassirer, 1940.
St.-John, Spenser. *Life in the Forests of the Far East*. London, UK: Smith, Elder, and Company, 1862.
Stadtmüller, Georg. *Die Kultur des Alten Russland*. Munich, Germany: Oldenbourg, 1950.
Stashower, Daniel. *Teller of Tales: The Life of Arthur Conan Doyle*. New York: Henry Holt and Company, 1999.
Stephens, Thomas. *The Literature of the Kymry*. London, UK: Longman, Green, Longman, Roberts, and Green, 1876.
Stevan Davies. *The Gospel of Thomas and Christian Wisdom*. New York: Seabury Press, 1983.
Strabo. *The Geography of Strabo*. London, UK: George Bell and Sons, 1903.
Strong, John S. *The Legend of King Aśoka: A Study and Translation of the Aśokāvadāna*. Princeton, NJ: Princeton University Press, 1983.
Suetonius, Gaius Tranquillus. *The Lives of the Caesars*. J. C. Rolfe, trans. New York: G. P. Putnam's Sons, 1913.
——. *The Twelve Caesars*. Robert Graves, trans. London, UK: Penguin Books, 1957.
Sukenik, Eleazar Lipa. *The Dead Sea Scrolls of the Hebrew University*. Jerusalem: Hebrew University Press, 1955.
Sullivan, Edward, ed. *The Book of Kells: A Selection of Pages Reproduced with an Introduction and Notes*. London, UK: The Studio, 1914.
Sullivan, George. *The Lost Treasures of Europe*. New York: American Heritage Press, 1967.
Sullivan, Jack. *Lost Treasure of the Superstitions*. Tucson, AZ: Southwest Publishing, 1975.
Symonds, John Addington. *Studies of the Greek Poets*. London, UK: Smith, Elder and Company, 1873.
Symons, Julian. *Arthur Conan Doyle: A Biography*. London, UK: Hamish Hamilton, 1979.
Tacitus, Cornelius. *Annals*. John Jackson, trans. London, UK: William Heinemann, 1937.
Tannenbaum, Samuel A. *The Editing of Shakespeare*. New York: Columbia University Press, 1928.
Taranatha. *History of Buddhism in India*. Lama Chimpa and Alaka Chattopadhyaya, trans. Calcutta, India: University of Calcutta, 1990.
Tarn, W. W. *Hellenistic Naval and Military Developments*. Cambridge, UK: Cambridge University Press, 1930.
Tarn, W. W. *Hellenistic Civilisation*. London, UK: Edward Arnold, 1927.
Taylor, John H., ed. *Journey Through the Afterlife: Ancient Egyptian Book of the Dead*. London, UK: British Museum Press, 2010.
Terry, Patricia. *The Song of the Nibelungs*. New York: Oxford University Press, 1969.
Thompson, J. Eric S. *Maya Hieroglyphic Writing: An Introduction*. Norman, OK: University of Oklahoma Press, 1950.
Thomson, Basil. *Savage Island: An Account of a Sojourn in Niué and Tonga*. London, UK: John Murray, 1902.
Thorkelin, Grímur Jónsson, ed. *De Danorum Rebus Gestis Secul. III & IV Poema Danicum Dialecto Anglosaxonica*. Copenhagen, Denmark: Typis Thielianis, 1815.
Thureau-Dangin, François. *Les Inscriptions de Sumer et d'Akkad*. Paris: Ernest Leroux, 1905.
Tilghman, Benjamin. *Treasures from Royal Courts of Europe*. London, UK: Faber and Faber, 1937.
Tischendorf, Constantin von. *The Discovery of the Sinaitic Manuscript*. London, UK: Bell and Daldy, 1860.

Torelli, Mario. *Studies in the Romanization of Etruria*. Berkeley, CA: University of California Press, 1995.
Townsend, Camilla. *Fifth Sun: A New History of the Aztecs*. Oxford, UK: Oxford University Press, 2019.
Toy, Crawford Howell. *Judaism and Christianity*. Boston, MA: Little, Brown, and Company, 1890.
Tozer, Henry Fanshawe, trans. *A Selection from Strabo*. Oxford, UK: Clarendon Press, 1895.
Tozer, Henry Fanshawe. *Selections from Strabo*. Oxford, UK: Clarendon Press, 1893.
Tozzer, Alfred M., trans. and ed. *Landa's Relación de las Cosas de Yucatán*. Cambridge, MA: Peabody Museum of American Archaeology and Ethnology, 1941.
Tregelles, Samuel P. *An Account of the Printed Text of the Greek New Testament*. London, UK: Samuel Bagster and Sons, 1854.
—. *An Introduction to the Critical Study and Knowledge of the Holy Scriptures*. London, UK: Samuel Bagster and Sons, 1856.
Trever, John C. *The Discovery of the Dead Sea Scrolls*. London, UK: Sheldon Press, 1965.
Tsukamoto, Zenryu. *A History of Early Buddhist Art and Literature*. Tokyo: Kodansha, 1985.
Turner, John D. *Sethian Gnosticism and the Platonic Tradition*. Waterloo, Ontario: Wilfrid Laurier University Press, 2001.
Turner, Ralph. *The Celtic Realms*. London, UK: Weidenfeld and Nicolson, 1967.
Turville-Petre, Gabriel. *Origins of Icelandic Literature*. Oxford, UK: Clarendon Press, 1953.
United States War Department. *Report on the Merkers Mine Treasure*. Washington, D.C.: Government Printing Office, 1945.
Upton-Ward, J. M., trans. *The Rule of the Templars*. Woodbridge, UK: Boydell Press, 1992.
Vaillant, George C. *The Aztecs of Mexico: Origin, Rise, and Fall of the Aztec Nation*. Garden City, NY: Doubleday, 1941.
Vebæk, Christian L. *The Norse Ruins of Igaliku*. Copenhagen, Denmark: The National Museum of Denmark, 1991.
Vermes, Géza. *Christian Beginnings: From Nazareth to Nicaea*. London, UK: Penguin Books, 2012.
Vielhauer, Philip. "Jewish Christian Gospels." In *New Testament Apocrypha: Volume One*, Wilhelm Schneemelcher, ed. Louisville, KY: Westminster John Knox Press, 1991.
Vielhauer, Philipp and George Ogg (eds.). *Earliest Christian Writings: Gospels, Apocalypses, and Related Literature*. Philadelphia, PA: Fortress Press, 1987.
Voigt, Eva-Maria, ed. *Sappho et Alcaeus: Fragmenta*. Amsterdam, Netherlands: Athenaeum–Polak and Van Gennep, 1971.
Vuolo, M. M. *The Master of the Temple*. Rome, Italy: Istituto Storico Italiano per il Medio Evo, 1960.
Wagner, Richard. *Wieland der Schmied: Studien zur Nibelungensage*. Leipzig, Germany: Breitkopf und Härtel, 1897.
Wakelyn, Jon L. *Jefferson Davis and the Civil War Era*. New York: University Press of America, 1983.
Wallis, James. *A Description of the Islands in the Pacific Ocean*. London, UK: Sherwood, Neely, and Jones, 1821.
Wanley, Humfrey. *Librorum Veterum Septentrionalium Catalogus*. Oxford, UK: E Theatro Sheldoniano, 1705.
Ward, Adolphus William. *English Dramatic Literature in the Reign of James I*. London, UK: Macmillan and Company, 1899.
Weidenreich, Franz. *The "Giant Early Man" from Asia*. Chicago, IL: University of Chicago Press, 1943.
Wellhausen, Julius. *Prolegomena to the History of Ancient Israel*. Edinburgh, Scotland: Adam and Charles Black, 1885.
Wells, Stanley and Gary Taylor. *William Shakespeare: A Textual Companion*. Oxford, UK:

Clarendon Press, 1987.
Wenn, Johannes. *Die Nibelungensage und der historische Hintergrund*. Munich, Germany: C. H. Beck, 1914.
Westcott, Brooke Foss, and Fenton John Anthony Hort, eds. *The New Testament in the Original Greek*. London, UK: Macmillan, 1881.
Westcott, Brooke Foss. *The Gospel of the Resurrection*. London, UK: Macmillan and Company, 1866.
Westwood, John Obadiah. *Fac-similes of the Miniatures and Ornaments of Anglo-Saxon and Irish Manuscripts*. London, UK: Bernard Quaritch, 1868.
Whaley, Diana. *Sagas of Icelanders: A Book of Essays*. New York: Garland Publishing, 1996.
Wharton, W. J. L. *Hydrographical Surveys of the Pacific and Adjacent Waters*. London, UK: Royal Navy Hydrographic Office, 1891.
Wheeler, Mortimer. *The Iron Age in Britain*. London, UK: Oxford University Press, 1935.
——. *Rome Beyond the Imperial Frontiers*. Harmondsworth, UK: Penguin Books, 1955.
Wilcken, Ulrich. *Griechische Geschichte im Rahmen der Altertumsgeschichte: Zweiter Band, Die hellenistische Zeit*. Berlin, Germany: Weidmannsche Buchhandlung, 1902.
Williams, Robert. *Enwogion Cymru: A Biographical Dictionary of Eminent Men of North Wales*. London, UK: W. Rees, 1852.
Williams, John (ed.). *Collectanea de Rebus Albanicis: Consisting of Original Papers and Documents Relating to the History of the Highlands and Islands of Scotland, and Particularly of the Clan MacDonald*. Edinburgh, Scotland: Maitland Club, 1847.
Williams, Glyndwr. *The Death of Captain Cook: A Hero Made and Unmade*. Cambridge, UK: Harvard University Press, 2008.
Williams, Gwyn A. *When Was Wales? A History of the Welsh*. London, UK: Penguin Books, 1985.
Wood, Bernard and Mark Collard. *Human Evolution: A Very Short Introduction*. Oxford, UK: Oxford University Press, 2014.
Woolf, Greg. *Becoming Roman: The Origins of Provincial Civilization in Gaul*. Cambridge, UK: Cambridge University Press, 1998.
Woolley, Leonard. *The Sumerians*. Oxford, UK: Clarendon Press, 1929.
Woolliscroft, D. J. *Roman Military Signalling*. Stroud, UK: Tempus Publishing, 2001.
Wrenn, C. L. and W. F. Bolton (eds.). *Beowulf: With the Finnesburg Fragment*. London, UK: Harrap and Co., 1953.
Wright, George Ernest. *Biblical Archaeology*. Philadelphia, PA: Westminster Press, 1957.
Wright, Michael T. *The Antikythera Mechanism and the Early History of Greek Mechanology*. London, UK: Imperial College Publications, 2005.
Xerez, Francisco de. *The Conquest of Peru*. In *The Narrative of the Conquest of Peru*. Clements R. Markham, ed. London, UK: Hakluyt Society, 1872.
Yadin, Yigael. *The Message of the Scrolls*. New York: Simon and Schuster, 1957.
Yamanaka, Akihide. *Nihontō: The Art of the Japanese Sword*. Tokyo: Sword Museum Press, 1958.
Yijing. *Buddhist Pilgrims in India and Java*. J. Takakusu, trans. Delhi, India: Motilal Banarsidass, 2005.
Yudin, Vladimir. *Altai Prehistory: The Peoples of the Siberian Highlands*. Moscow, Russia: Academy of Sciences Press, 1962.
Zangwill, Israel. *Children of the Ghetto: A Study of a Peculiar People*. Philadelphia, PA: The Jewish Publication Society of America, 1892.
Zimmer, Carl. *She Has Her Mother's Laugh: The Powers, Perversions, and Potential of Heredity*. New York: Dutton, 2018.
Zosimus. *Historia Nova*. Ronald T. Ridley, trans. Sydney, Australia: Australian Association for Byzantine Studies, 1982.

MEET THE AUTHOR

LOCHLAINN SEABROOK, who has been described as "a Humboldt-Kircher polymath, with da Vinci's integrative creativity, Benjamin Franklin's productivity, Thomas Jefferson's intellectual breadth, and Linnaeus's system-building architecture," is a prolific lifelong researcher, historian, author, artist, and composer whose knowledge and experience span numerous fields. His remarkable productivity arises from this broad foundation, as well as decades of meticulous research and an unwavering daily devotion to writing and creative exploration.

The idea of specializing in a single subject is a modern invention. In the spirit of the great polymaths—Aristotle, Isaac Newton, Benjamin Franklin, and Thomas Jefferson—Seabrook works across dozens of disciplines with intellectual pursuits encompassing history, science, philosophy, religion, and the arts. The result is an expansive body of original writings that distill years of careful analysis into clear, accessible language for the general reader.

Rejecting the narrow confines of modern specialization, Seabrook views all knowledge as intrinsically interconnected. This integrative vision, combined with long hours of focused, solitary study and a rigorous work ethic, has enabled him to produce an extraordinary corpus of literature uniting the sciences and the humanities—a natural outgrowth of a lifetime devoted to inquiry, creativity, and the presentation of evidence-based history.

AMERICAN POLYMATH LOCHLAINN SEABROOK is a bestselling author, award-winning historian, and acclaimed multidisciplinary artist. A descendant of the families of Alexander Hamilton Stephens, John Singleton Mosby, Edmund Winchester Rucker, and William Giles Harding, the neo-Victorian scholar is a 7th generation Kentuckian, and one of the most prolific and widely read traditional writers in the world today. Known by literary critics as the "new Shelby Foote," the "American Robert Graves," the "Southern Joseph Campbell," and the "Rocky Mountain Richard Jefferies," and by his fans as the "the best author ever," he is a recipient of the United Daughters of the Confederacy's prestigious Jefferson Davis Historical Gold Medal, and is considered the foremost Southern interpreter of American Civil War history—or what he refers to as the War for the Constitution (1861-1865).

A lifelong litterateur, the Sons of Confederate Veterans member has authored and edited books ranging in topics from ancient and modern history, politics, science, comparative religion, diet and nutrition, spirituality, astronomy, entertainment, military, biography, mysticism, anthropology, cryptozoology, photography, and Bible studies, to natural history, technology, paleography, music, humor, gastronomy, etymology, paleontology, onomastics, mysteries, alternative health and fitness, wildlife, alternate history, comparative mythology, genealogy, Christian history, and the paranormal; books that his readers describe as "game changers," "transformative," and "life altering."

One of America's most popular living historians, nature writers, autodidacts, and Transcendentalists, he is a 17th generation Southerner of Appalachian heritage who descends from dozens of patriotic Revolutionary War soldiers and Confederate soldiers from Kentucky, Tennessee, North Carolina, and Virginia. Also a history, wildlife, and nature preservationist, the well-respected scrivener began life as a child prodigy, later maturing into an archetypal Renaissance Man and classical cross-modal polymath.

Besides being cofounder and co-CEO of Sea Raven Press, an accomplished writer, author, historian, biographer, lexicographer, encyclopedist, neologist, publisher, editor, poet, polymathic creative, onomastician, etymologist, and Bible authority, the influential prosateur is also a Kentucky Colonel, eagle scout, entrepreneur, businessman, composer, screenwriter, nature, wildlife, and landscape photographer, videographer, and filmmaker, artist, artisan, art director, painter, watercolorist, sculptor, ceramic artist, visual artist, sketch artist, pen and ink artist, graphic artist, graphic designer, book designer, book formatter, editorial designer, book cover designer, publishing designer, Web designer, poster artist, digital artist, cartoonist, content creator, inventor, aquarist, genealogist, ufologist, jewelry designer, jewelry maker, former history museum docent, teacher's assistant, and a former Red Cross certified lifeguard, ranch hand, zookeeper, and wrangler. A contemporary songwriter (of some 3,000 songs in a dozen genres), he is also a pianist, organist, drummer, bass player, rhythm guitarist, rhythm mandolinist, percussionist, electronic musician, synthesist, clavichordist, harpsichordist, classical composer, jingle composer, film composer (currently his musical work has been featured in 11 movies), lyricist, band leader, multi-instrument musician, lead vocalist, backup vocalist, session player, music producer, and recording studio mixing engineer, who has worked and performed with some of Nashville's top musicians and singers.

Currently Seabrook is the multi-genre author and editor of over 100 adult and children's books (totaling some 30,000 pages and 15,000,000 words) that have earned him accolades from around the globe. His works, which have sold on every continent except Antarctica, have introduced hundreds of thousands to vital facts that have been left out of our mainstream books. He has been endorsed internationally by leading experts, museum curators, award-winning historians, chart-topping authors, celebrities, filmmakers, noted scientists, well regarded educators, TV show hosts and producers, renowned military artists, venerable heritage organizations, and distinguished academicians of all races, creeds, and colors.

He currently holds two interesting world records: He is the author of the most books on American military officer Nathan Bedford Forrest, and he was the first to publicize and describe the 19th-Century platform reversal of America's two main political parties, namely that Civil War era Democrats (primarily in the South—the Confederacy) were Conservatives, while Civil War era Republicans (primarily in the North—the Union) were Liberals.

Of northern, western, and central European ancestry, he is the 6th great-grandson of the Earl of Oxford and a descendant of European royalty through his Kentucky father and West Virginia mother. A proud descendant of Appalachian coal miners, trainmen, mountain folk, and wilderness pioneers, his modern day cousins include: Johnny Cash, Elvis Presley, Lisa Marie Presley, Billy Ray and Miley Cyrus, Patty Loveless, Tim McGraw, Lee Ann Womack, Dolly Parton, Pat Boone, Naomi, Wynonna, and Ashley Judd, Ricky Skaggs, the Sunshine Sisters, Martha Carson, Chet Atkins, Patrick J. Buchanan, Cindy Crawford, Bertram Thomas Combs (Kentucky's 50th governor), Edith Bolling (second wife of President Woodrow Wilson), Andy Griffith, Riley Keough, George C. Scott, Robert Duvall, Reese Witherspoon, Lee Marvin, Rebecca Gayheart, and Tom Cruise.

A constitutionalist, avid outdoorsman, wilderness conservationist, and gun rights advocate, Seabrook is the author of the international blockbuster, *Everything You Were Taught About the Civil War is Wrong, Ask a Southerner!* He lives with his wife and family in the magnificent Rocky Mountains, heart of the American West, where you will find him writing, hiking, and filming.

For more information on Mr. Seabrook visit
LochlainnSeabrook.com

Praise for Author-Historian-Artist
Lochlainn Seabrook

"Bestselling author, award-winning historian, and esteemed nature writer Lochlainn Seabrook straddles multiple genres with ease, seamlessly weaving together history, science, politics, philosophy, and spirituality with the authority of a scholar and the flair of a storyteller." — SEA RAVEN PRESS

COMMENTS FROM OUR READERS AROUND THE WORLD

★ "Lochlainn Seabrook is a genius writer!" — STEVEN WARD

★ "Best author ever." — EMILY

★ "We get asked a lot what books we use and read. We don't do many modern historians, but we make an exception for some, and Lochlainn Seabrook is one of them. His works are completely well researched from original documents, and heavily footnoted and documented." — SOUTHERN HISTORICAL SOCIETY

★ "Looking forward to more Lochlainn Seabrook books, my favourite historian!" — ALBERTO IGLESIAS

★ "Lochlainn Seabrook is one of the finest authors on true history in this century. His books should be on every student's desk." — RONDA SAMMONS RENO

★ "All of Col. Seabrook's books are great. I have bought most of them and want to end up buying them all." — DAVID VAUGHN

★ "Lochlainn pulls together such arcane facts with relative ease, compiling these into ordinary prose that strike to the heart with substance, no fluff-speak. I am awestruck! Really. He is an inspiration to me. . . . He is truly a revolutionist. He dares to speak what others whisper; he writes with a boldness and an authoritative knowledge that is second to none." — JAY KRUIZENGA

★ "Mr. Lochlainn Seabrook is . . . the most well researched and heavily documented author I've ever read. His books are must haves. Everything he writes should be required reading! I assure you, you won't be disappointed. One simply cannot go wrong with his books. Mr. Seabrook is awesome! . . . I have never read any other author as well researched and footnoted as him. I've been in love with Mr. Seabrook for almost 5 years now. His quick wit and logic is enough reason to purchase his books. But the mere fact that he's so extensively researched is icing on the cake. Mr. Seabrook is my favorite, hands down." — LANI BURNETTE RINKEL

★ "My favorite book is the Bible. Lochlainn Seabrook wrote my second favorite book." — RICHARD FINGER

★ "I have a new favorite author and his name is Lochlainn Seabrook." — J. EWING

★ "Lochlainn Seabrook is an incredible writer and I love all of his books on the South. . . . His writing is brilliant. . . . I look forward to reading more of his masterpieces. Thank you." — JOEY

★ "It's hard to choose just one of Lochlainn's books!" — ROSANNE STEELE

★ "Mr. Seabrook, thank you ever so much for blessing us with your most enlightening works." — LAURENCE DRURY

★ "I recommend anything written by Lochlainn Seabrook." — HOTRODMOB

★ "Awesome books . . . by a great writer of truth, Lochlainn. Thank you so much. Keep up the great work you do." — WILDBUNCH19INF

★ "I love Lochlainn Seabrook's style and approach. It's not the 'norm.' What a miracle his books are. . . . He is a literal life changing author! Amazing books!" — KEITH PARISH

★ "I adore Mr. Seabrook's style and I love his books. I love an author that does proper research, and still finds a way to engage the reader. Mr. Seabrook does an admirable job of both." — DONALD CAUL

★ "Lochlainn Seabrook's books are much more well researched and authoritative than those eminently celebrated as being the authorities on the subjects he writes on. You can always trust to find the truth in his writings. . . . He does not rewrite history, but instead shows it as it is." — GARY STIER

★ "I love all of Colonel Seabrook's books. They are informative and enlightening, and his warm Southern hospitality writing style makes you feel right at home." — KEITH CRAVEN

★ "Lochlainn Seabrook's work is an absolute treasure of scholarship and historic scope." — MARK WAYNE CUNNINGHAM

★ "Mr. Seabrook's command of . . . history is breathtaking. . . . He deserves great renown—check out his books!" — MARGARET SIMMONS

★ "I love Seabrook's writings. LOVE!!! . . . So grateful to know the truth! Keep writing Lochlainn!!!" — REBECCA DALRYMPLE

★ "Lochlainn Seabrook . . . [has] probably [written] the best book on mental science in existence by a living author. Along with Thomas Troward, Emmet Fox, and Jack Addington, Mr. Seabrook is one of the top four mental science authors of all time, since biblical times." - IAN BARTON STEWART

★ "Glad I discovered Mr. Seabrook! . . . He writes eye opening books! Unbelievable the facts he unearths - and he backs it all up with truth, notes, footnotes, and bibliography! . . . He always amazes me! His books always see the whole picture. His timelines and bibliographies are incredible. He always provides carefully reasoned arguments! He's the best. To me I think he's better than the late great Shelby Foote! America needs more like Lochlainn Seabrook. I can't wait to own all of his books on the war someday. Everyone who wants the Truth, who seeks the Truth and wants the full story, should read his books." — JOHN BULL BADER

★ "I love all of Colonel Seabrook's books!" — DEBBIE SIDLE

★ "Amazing books for unreconstructed people who actually want to know the TRUTH. Seabrook's skill in writing and researching has no equal since the great Shelby Foote. If I could rate his books more than five stars I would." — CANDICE

★ "Lochlainn Seabrook is well educated and versed in what he writes and I'm impressed with the delivery." — THOMAS L. WHITE

★ "Lochlainn Seabrook is the author of great works of scholarship." — JOHN B.

★ "Thank you Lochlainn Seabrook for your wonderful books! You are the real deal! You are an amazing author and I love your books!!" — SOPHIA MEOW CELLIST

★ "I really enjoy Mr. Seabrook's books! His knowledge is beyond belief!" — SANDRA FISH

★ "Love Lochlainn Seabrook. Awesome!!" — ROBIN HENDERSON ARISTIDES

★ "Kudos to Lochlainn Seabrook who is a very good and informative professional truthful historian. We need more like him!" — AMY VACHON

Nurture Your Mind, Body, and Spirit!

READ THE BOOKS OF

SEA RAVEN PRESS

Visit our Webstore for a wide selection of wholesome, family-friendly, evidence-based, educational books for all ages. You'll be glad you did!

Artisan-Crafted Books & Merch From the Rocky Mountains

THANK YOU FOR SUPPORTING OUR SMALL AMERICAN FAMILY BUSINESS!

SeaRavenPress.com

Visit our sister sites:
LochlainnSeabrook.com
YouTube.com/user/SeaRavenPress
YouTube.com/@SeabrookFilms
Rumble.com/user/SeaRavenPress
Pond5.com/artist/LochlainnSeabrook

If you enjoyed this book you will be interested in some of Colonel Seabrook's other popular titles:

☛ The 50 Most Beautiful Aquarium Fish in the World: An Illustrated Guide to Nature's Most Stunning Freshwater and Marines Species
☛ The Gospel of Thomas: A Christian Mystic's View of Christianity's Most Important Ancient Text
☛ The Cryptid Files Unsealed: An Illustrated Guide to the World's Most Terrifying Unknown Creatures
☛ The Greatest Jesus Mystery of All Time: Where Was Christ Between the Ages of 12 and 30?
☛ When Monsters Ruled: The 25 Scariest Animals of the Prehistoric World
☛ Jesus and the Gospel of Q: Christ's Pre-Christian Teachings as Recorded in the New Testament
☛ Seabrook's Bible Dictionary of Traditional and Mystical Christian Doctrines
☛ Manmade: Male Inventors Who Created the Modern World

Available from Sea Raven Press and wherever fine books are sold

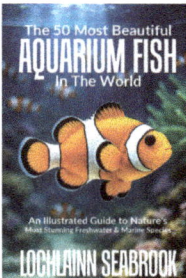
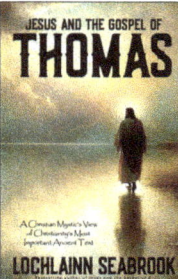
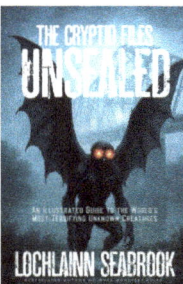

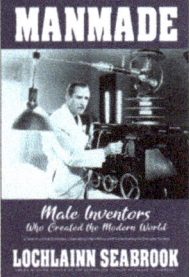

PLEASE VISIT OUR WEBSTORE FOR A COMPLETE LIST OF COLONEL SEABROOK'S BOOKS, AS WELL AS HIS FINE ART NATURE & WILDLIFE PHOTO PRINTS, POSTERS, AND BUMPER STICKERS

SeaRavenPress.com

www.ingramcontent.com/pod-product-compliance
Lightning Source LLC
Chambersburg PA
CBHW040227180426
43200CB00026BA/2948